Contents
Inhalt
Sommaire
Contenido

Published by: Lily Publications, PO Box 33, Ramsey, Isle of Man IM99 4LP
Tel: +44 (0) 1624 898446 Fax: +44 (0) 1624 898449
E-mail: info@lilypublications.co.uk
www.lilypublications.co.uk
© 2016. All rights reserved.

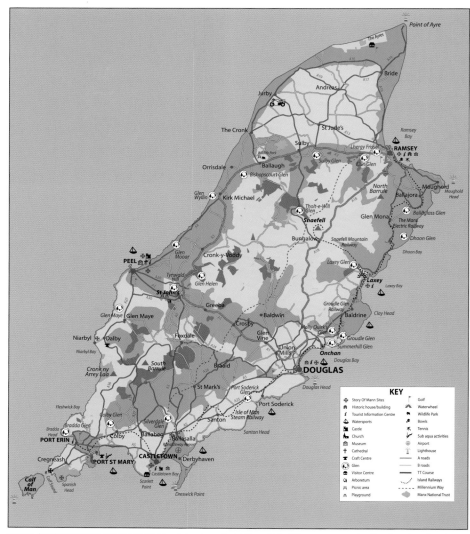

KEY

✛	Story Of Mann Sites	⌐	Golf
⌂	Historic house/building	☀	Waterwheel
i	Tourist Information Centre	♦	Wildlife Park
⚓	Watersports	♣	Bowls
⌂	Castle	✗	Tennis
⛪	Church		Sub aqua activities
⌂	Museum	✈	Airport
✝	Cathedral	☀	Lighthouse
✗	Craft Centre	——	A roads
⊙	Glen	——	B roads
⌂	Visitor Centre	——	TT Course
♧	Arboretum	⋯⋯	Island Railways
⚘	Picnic area	- - - -	Millennium Way
⚐	Playground		Manx National Trust

Welcome to the Isle of Man

Nestled in the Irish Sea, midway between Britain and Ireland, the Isle of Man is a haven for the good life. Popular for its wildlife, water sports, motorsports and breathtaking scenery, it is still something of a hidden gem, with its quiet, unhurried lifestyle and great natural beauty being overlooked by many holidaymakers, making it one of the best kept secrets around.

During the Victorian tourism boom the Island was popular with workers from the British mainland escaping the drudgery of everyday life, then in the post-war years of the 1940s and 50s became a popular destination for many and has remained a favourite for those in the know ever since. Peer beneath Manannan's Cloak (a natural phenomena and mythological mechanism for hiding the Island from the world in times of trouble) and you will find an island, often unnoticed, that holds a wealth of history, beautiful unspoilt landscapes and a relaxed way of life that is both friendly and inviting.

Home to the oldest parliament in the world, ruling unbroken for over 1,000 years, the Isle of Man is steeped in history and heritage. Established by Norse settlers, Tynwald is a system of self-government that sets the Island apart from the British Isles, empowering Manx people to make their own laws and allowing them to remain independent while enjoying close relations with the UK. With their Celtic and Norse roots, and Gaelic language, a relaxed atmosphere pervades the Island encapsulated in the Manx saying traa dy-liooar, meaning 'time enough'.

Within the pages of this guide you will find all you need to know about the Isle of Man whilst visiting the Island for either TT, Southern 100 or the Festival of Motorcycling (formerly known as MGP).

Willkommen auf der Isle of Man

Mitten in der irischen See zwischen Großbritannien und Irland befindet sich die Isle of Man, ein herrliches Fleckchen voller Lebensqualität. Sie ist für ihre Flora und Fauna, Wassersport, Motorsport und atemberaubende Landschaft bekannt, trotzdem ist sie immer noch ein verstecktes Juwel. Ihre ruhige, gemütliche Lebensart und umwerfende Naturschönheit werden von vielen Urlaubern übersehen, so dass sie eines der bestgehüteten Geheimnisse ist.

Als der Tourismus im viktorianischen Zeitalter boomte, war die Insel besonders bei Arbeitern vom britischen Festland beliebt, die hier den Strapazen des Alltags entflohen. Später in der Nachkriegszeit der 1940er-50er wurde sie ein weithin beliebtes Reiseziel und ist nach wie vor eines der Lieblingsziele Eingeweihter. Schauen Sie unter Manannans Mantel (so heißt ein Naturphänomen, das der Legende nach die Insel in schweren Zeiten vor der Welt versteckt) und Sie entdecken eine oft übersehene Insel mit einer reichen Geschichte, unberührten Landschaften und einer freundlich-entspannten und einladenden Lebensart.

Auf der traditionsreichen Isle of Man gibt es das älteste Parlament der Welt, das seit über 1000 Jahren ohne Unterbrechung regiert. Das Tynwald wurde von norwegischen Siedlern gegründet und stellt eine Form der Selbstregierung dar, durch die sich die Insel von den übrigen britischen Inseln unterscheidet. So sind die Manx in der Lage, eigene Gesetze zu verabschieden, unabhängig zu bleiben und dennoch enge Beziehungen zum Vereinigten Königreich zu unterhalten. Auf der Insel mit ihren keltischen und norwegischen Wurzeln herrscht eine entspannte Atmosphäre. Die Manx bringen sie mit der gälischen Redewendung „traa dy-liooar", was „Zeit genug" bedeutet, auf den Punkt.

Dieser Reiseführer verrät Ihnen alles, was sie über die Isle of Man wissen müssen, wenn Sie die Insel anlässlich der TT, Southern 100 oder des Festival of Motorcycling (ehemals MPG) besuchen.

Bienvenue à l'Île de Man

Située en mer d'Irlande, à mi-chemin entre la Grande-Bretagne et l'Irlande, l'île de Man est un refuge de bien être. Célèbre pour sa faune et sa flore, ses sports aquatiques, automobiles et ses paysages à couper le souffle, ce trésor encore caché plein de quiétude avec son mode de vie tranquille et son extraordinaire beauté naturelle a été négligé par les vacanciers faisant de ce lieu un des secrets les mieux gardés de la région.

Durant l'essor du tourisme à l'ère victorienne, les ouvriers de Grande-Bretagne voulant échapper à leur quotidien difficile rendirent l'île populaire, puis, dans les années d'après-guerre et dans les années 40 et 50, elle devint pour beaucoup une destination prisée et est restée une destination privilégiée pour ceux qui la connaisse. Percez le fameux brouillard Manannan's Cloak (un phénomène naturel et un mécanisme mythologique pour protéger l'île du monde en période de troubles) et vous découvrirez une île souvent imperceptible au passé historique riche, avec de magnifiques paysages préservés et une douceur de vivre agréable et accueillante.

Abritant le plus ancien parlement du monde gouverné sans interruption depuis plus de 1 000 ans, l'île de Man est ancrée dans l'histoire et possède un riche héritage. Établi par les colons scandinaves, le Tynwald est un système d'autonomie gouvernementale qui distingue l'île des îles Britanniques permettant aux Manxois d'adopter leurs propres lois et de rester indépendants tout en profitant de relations étroites avec le Royaume-Uni. Bien enracinée dans sa culture celte et scandinave et avec sa langue gaélique, l'île dégage une ambiance détendue que l'on peut résumer par comme les Manxois le disent « traa dy-liooar » qui veut dire « assez de temps ».

Au fil des pages de ce guide, vous trouverez tout ce dont vous avez besoin pour découvrir l'Île de Man tout en visitant l'île que ce soit pour le TT, le Southern 100 ou le Festival de Moto de l'Île de Man (anciennement appelé le MGP).

Bienvenido a la Isla de Man

Enclavada en el mar de Irlanda, a medio camino entre Gran Bretaña e Irlanda, la Isla de Man es un paraíso del buen vivir. Su fauna y flora, la práctica de deportes acuáticos y de motor y sus imponentes paisajes gozan de gran popularidad, mientras que otros atractivos de la isla como su forma de vida relajada y pausada y su extraordinaria belleza natural son una suerte de tesoros ocultos que pasan inadvertidos a los ojos del común de los turistas, siendo así algunos de sus secretos mejor guardados.

Durante el boom turístico de la época victoriana la isla era frecuentada por la clase trabajadora de Gran Bretaña deseosa de escapar de la monotonía diaria; más tarde, en el periodo posterior a la Segunda Guerra Mundial (años 40 y 50), se convirtió en un destino muy popular, estatus que ha mantenido hasta nuestros días entre los conocedores de sus numerosos alicientes. Si escrutamos bajo la capa de niebla que la cubre, conocida como Manannan's Cloak (fenómeno natural a la par que conjuro mitológico según el cual la isla queda oculta del resto del mundo en épocas de tribulación), descubriremos lo que a algunos pasa desapercibido: una tierra cargada de historia, unos paisajes de intacta belleza y una forma de vida relajada, agradable y tentadora.

La Isla de Man, sede del parlamento más antiguo del mundo en funcionamiento ininterrumpido desde hace más de 1000 años, está llena de historia y herencia cultural. El Tynwald, instaurado por los primitivos pobladores vikingos, es un sistema de autogobierno que confiere a la isla autonomía respecto a las islas británicas, permitiendo a los maneses contar con su propia legislación, mantener su independencia y gozar a la vez de unas estrechas relaciones con el Reino Unido. La isla, que hunde sus raíces en la herencia nórdica y celta y cuyo idioma es el gaélico, disfruta de una relajada forma de vida resumida perfectamente en la expresión traa dy-liooar, que en gaélico manés significa "tiempo suficiente".

En las páginas de esta guía encontrará toda la información que pueda necesitar si visita la isla para asistir al Tourist Trophy (TT), la Southern 100 o el Festival of Motorcycling (antes conocido como MGP).

🇬🇧 Getting Around

Heritage Railways Scheduled Services (check for2017 schedule)
- **Isle of Man Steam Railway:** 4th March to 6th November 2016
- **Manx Electric Railway:** 18th March to 6th November 2016
- **Snaefell Mountain Railway:** 18th March to 6th November 2016

Bus Vannin
With regular operating bus services, getting around the Island could not be easier.

Timetables
Timetables are available from the Welcome Centre in Douglas Sea Terminal and main bus and rail stations, they are also available from www.iombusandrail.info or please call +44 (0) 1624 662525.

Multi-Journey Tickets
To help make your stay even more enjoyable and affordable, multi-journey tickets are available. Island Explorer Tickets (unlimited Travel on scheduled services of the Steam Railway, Manx Electric Railway and Snaefell Mountain Railway, Buses [except Manx Express]), Heritage Explorer Tickets (as Island Explorer but including entry to all Manx National Heritage Sites) and Saver Tickets (Unlimited Travel on scheduled bus services [except Manx Express]) are available from the Welcome Centre at the Sea Terminal, main bus and rail stations and selected ticket agents. To obtain tickets in advance of your visit, please call +44 (0) 1624 662525.

🇩🇪 Transport mittel

Fahrpläne historischer Eisenbahnen
- **Isle of Man Steam Railway:** März bis November
- **Manx Electric Railway:** März bis November
- **Snaefell Mountain Railway:** März bis November

Bus Vannin
Die regelmäßig fahrenden Busse sind die einfachste Art und Weise sich auf der Insel fortzubewegen.

Fahrpläne
Die Fahrpläne sind am Informationszentrum des Meeresbahnhofs in Douglas und an großen Bushaltestellen und Bahnhöfen sowie unter www.iombusandrail.info erhältlich. Gerne können Sie auch unter der Nummer +44 (0) 1624 662525 anrufen.

Mehrfahrtenkarten
Damit Ihr Aufenthalt noch sorgloser und günstiger wird, werden auch Mehrfahrtenkarten angeboten. Am Informationszentrum des Meeresbahnhofs und an großen Bushaltestellen und Bahnhöfen sowie bei ausgewählten Fahrkartenverkäufern sind Island Explorer Tickets (unbegrenztes Fahren mit planmäßigen Fahrten der Isle of Man Steam Railway, Manx Electric Railway und Snaefell Mountain Railway, Buses [außer Manx Express]), Heritage Explorer

Tickets (wie Island Explorer Tickets, aber inklusive Eintritt in alle Kulturerbestätten der Insel) und Saver Tickets (unbegrenztes Fahren mit allen planmäßigen Buslinien [außer Manx Express]) erhältlich. Um vor Ihrem Besuch Karten zu erwerben, rufen Sie bitte unter +44 (0) 1624 662525 an.

▪▪ Déplacement

Services réguliers Heritage Railways
- **Chemin de fer à vapeur de l'Île de Man:** de mars à novembre
- **Chemin de fer électrique manxois:** de mars à novembre
- **Chemin de fer de montagne du Snaefell:** de mars à novembre

Bus Vannin
Vous ne pouvez être mieux desservis qu'avec les services réguliers par bus pour sillonner l'île.

Horaires
Les horaires sont disponibles au Centre d'accueil de la gare maritime de Douglas et dans les gares routières et ferroviaires principales, ils peuvent également être consultés sur www.iombusandrail.info, demandés par téléphone au +44 (0) 1624 662525.

Billets pour trajets multiples
Des billets de trajets multiples sont à votre disposition pour contribuer à rendre votre séjour encore plus agréable et abordable. Les billets Island Explorer (trajets illimités en services réguliers du chemin de fer à vapeur, du chemin de fer électrique manxois et du chemin de fer de montagne du Snaefell, bus de Douglas [sauf Manx Express]), les billets Heritage Explorer (comme les Island Explorer mais avec l'entrée dans tous les sites du patrimoine national de l'Île de Man [Manx National Heritage]) et les billets Saver (trajets illimités en services réguliers de bus [sauf Manx Express]) sont disponibles au Centre d'accueil de la gare maritime, dans les gares routières et ferroviaires principales et auprès de billetteries sélectionnées. Veuillez appeler le +44 (0) 1624 662525 pour obtenir des tickets avant votre séjour.

Transporte en la Isla

Servicios regulares de Heritage Railways
- **Isle of Man Steam Railway:** marzo a noviembre.
- **Manx Electric Railway:** marzo a noviembre.
- **Snaefell Mountain Railway:** marzo a noviembre.

Bus Vannin
Sus servicios de autobús regulares permiten desplazarse fácilmente por la isla.

Horarios
Los horarios pueden obtenerse en el centro de bienvenida de la terminal marítima de Douglas, en las principales estaciones de autobuses y ferrocarril, accediendo a www.iombusandrail.info o bien llamando al teléfono +44 (0) 1624 662525.

Billetes multiviaje
Tiene la posibilidad de adquirir títulos multiviaje para que su estancia resulte más agradable y asequible. Las modalidades de billete Island Explorer (viajes ilimitados en servicios regulares del ferrocarril de vapor, del tranvía eléctrico de la Isla de Man, del ferrocarril del monte Snaefell, y de autobuses [salvo el Manx Express]), Heritage Explorer (igual que el Island Explorer pero con acceso a la totalidad de sitios del Patrimonio Nacional manés) y Saver (viajes ilimitados en servicios regulares de autobús [salvo el Manx Express]) pueden adquirirse en el centro de bienvenida de la terminal marítima, en las principales estaciones de autobuses y ferrocarril así como en puntos de venta seleccionados. Si desea adquirir sus billetes antes de su llegada, llame al teléfono +44 (0) 1624 662525.

Sulby Crossroads

Important information

A one-way system is in operation over the Mountain Road for the TT Festival, from the Ramsey Hairpin to the Creg Ny Baa for the whole of the TT Festival.

The TT course uses public roads, so when the races are in action, these roads are closed. It is important to remember that when the roads are open both residents and visitors use the same sections of the course for their day-to-day activities. Be prepared for regular traffic on the TT course including queues at roundabouts and junctions.

Do not use unacceptable speeds on long stretches of road, and always drive within your capabilities and be aware of your surroundings. Isle of Man roads are often narrow and winding with limited visibility, so be aware of what you are doing.

On right hand bends you must ensure that both you and your machine are behind the white line and not just your tyres.

Many visitors may not be used to riding on the left hand side of the road. Please take extra care when approaching areas where their journey might start, like campsites.

Temporary speed limits will be introduced to cope with the increased volume of traffic. These are in place to improve safety for all road users.

Driving bans imposed by an Isle of Man Court also apply in the UK as there is a reciprocal ban agreement in place.

If you are going to enjoy the local beer please leave your bike where you are staying. Alternatively stick to a soft drink as riding, alcohol and unfamiliar roads do not mix.

www.respectourroads.im

Remember, where this sign is displayed it is prohibited to spectate in the area. This is for your own safety and the safety of the riders.

Wichtige Informationen

Während des gesamten TT Festivals gilt auf der Bergstraße von der Haarnadelkurve Ramsey Hairpin bis zur Creg-Ny-Baa-Kreuzung eine Einbahnregelung.

Die TT-Rennstrecke verläuft über öffentliche Straßen, diese sind gesperrt, während die Rennen stattfinden. Beachten Sie, dass sowohl Anwohner als auch Besucher dieselben Streckenabschnitte verwenden, wenn die Straßen offen sind. Deswegen ist mit hohem Verkehrsaufkommen auf der TT-Strecke einschließlich Staus an Verkehrskreiseln und Kreuzungen zu rechnen.

Fahren Sie auf langen Straßenabschnitten nicht mit überhöhter Geschwindigkeit, überschätzen Sie Ihre Fähigkeiten nicht und achten Sie auf Ihre Umgebung. Die Straßen auf der Isle of Man sind oft schmal und gewunden, so dass die Sicht eingeschränkt ist. Bitte fahren Sie deshalb mit Bedacht.

Achten Sie bei Rechtskurven darauf, dass Sie und das gesamte Fahrzeug hinter der weißen Linie bleiben und nicht nur die Räder.

Viele Besucher sind nicht daran gewöhnt, auf der linken Straßenseite zu fahren. Seien Sie deshalb bitte an Stellen, wo sich möglicherweise Besucher dem Verkehr anschließen, wie an Campingplätzen, besonders vorsichtig.

Um das erhöhte Verkehrsaufkommen zu bewältigen,

werden vorübergehende Geschwindigkeitsbegrenzungen eingeführt. Sie dienen dazu, die Sicherheit aller Verkehrsteilnehmer zu gewährleisten.

Fahrverbote, die von einem Gericht der Isle of Man verhängt werden, gelten auch in Großbritannien, da es hierzu eine gegenseitige Abmachung gibt.

Wenn Sie das einheimische Bier probieren, lassen Sie Ihr Motorrad bitte an Ihrer Unterkunft. Oder bleiben Sie bei alkoholfreien Getränken – denn Fahren, Alkohol und unbekannte Straßen sind eine schlechte Kombination.

www.respectourroads.im

In Bereichen, in denen dieses Schild angebracht ist, ist das Zuschauen nicht gestattet. Dies dient Ihrer Sicherheit und der der Fahrer.

Information importante

Un système d'aller simple fonctionne sur la Mountain Road du Festival TT, de Ramsey Hairpin à Creg Ny Baa pendant toute la durée du Festival TT.

L'évènement TT se fait sur la voie publique, si bien que lorsque des courses ont lieu, les routes empruntées sont fermées. Il est important de se rappeler que lorsque les routes sont ouvertes, les résidents et visiteurs empruntent les mêmes portions de course pour leurs activités quotidiennes. Préparez-vous à faire la queue aux ronds points et intersections lorsque le trafic sur le circuit TT est régulier.

Ne roulez pas à une vitesse excessive sur les longs trajets sur route, et roulez toujours en fonction de vos capacités et en étant conscient de ce qui vous entoure. Les routes de l'Île de Man sont souvent étroites et sinueuses avec une visibilité limitée, soyez donc conscients de ce que vous faites.

Dans les virages à droite, vous devez vous assurer que vous et la machine se trouvent derrière la ligne blanche et pas seulement les pneus.

Beaucoup de visiteurs ne connaissent pas la conduite à gauche sur la route. Veuillez également faire preuve de prudence aux abords de zones de séjour telles que des campings.

Les limitations de vitesse temporaires seront appliquées pour faire face à l'augmentation de la densité du trafic. Elles sont mises en place pour améliorer la sécurité de tous les usagers de la route.

Des interdictions de circulation instaurées par la Cour de l'Île de Man sont applicables également au Royaume-Uni étant donné qu'il existe un accord réciproque d'interdiction en vigueur.

Si vous voulez profiter de la bière locale, laissez votre moto où vous séjournez. Sinon, il est préférable de prendre une boisson sans alcool lorsque l'on conduit, l'alcool et les routes inconnues ne font pas bon ménage.

www.respectourroads.im

Rappelez-vous que lorsque ce panneau est affiché, il est strictement interdit de suivre la course dans la zone. Il s'agit d'une mesure de sécurité qui vise à vous protéger ainsi que les motocyclistes.

Información importante

Durante la celebración del TT Festival, la carretera de la montaña se habilita para circular en un único sentido en el tramo desde Ramsey Hairpin a Creg Ny Baa.

El trazado del TT discurre por vías públicas que se cierran al tráfico con motivo de la competición. Es importante recordar que cuando las carreteras están abiertas al público, tanto los residentes como los visitantes circulan por el propio trazado del circuito para sus actividades diarias. Tenga presente que encontrará tráfico en el trazado del TT, incluyendo colas en rotondas e intersecciones.

No conduzca a velocidades inaceptables en largos tramos de vía; hágalo siempre dentro de sus capacidades y esté alerta con lo que sucede a su alrededor. Las vías rodadas de la Isla de Man son con frecuencia estrechas, sinuosas y de limitada visibilidad; por tanto, esté atento a lo que hace.

Asegúrese de que tanto sus neumáticos como su cuerpo y su moto se encuentren por detrás de la línea blanca en las curvas de derechas.

Muchos visitantes carecen de experiencia conduciendo por el lado izquierdo de la carretera. Extreme las precauciones cuando se aproxime a posibles puntos de inicio de desplazamientos, como es el caso de los campings.

Durante la competición se aplican límites de velocidad temporales a fin de hacer frente al incremento del tráfico. Estas limitaciones pretenden mejorar la seguridad de todos los usuarios de las vías de la isla.

Las prohibiciones de circular impuestas por los tribunales de la Isla de Man son aplicables también en el Reino Unido en virtud del acuerdo de reciprocidad suscrito por ambas partes.

Si piensa disfrutar de la cerveza local, no saque su moto. Si decide conducir, consuma únicamente bebidas sin alcohol; la conducción, el alcohol y las carreteras desconocidas forman una pésima combinación.

www.respectourroads.im

Recuerde que esta señal indica que se encuentra en una zona prohibida para seguir las carreras. Se trata de una medida encaminada a salvaguardar tanto su integridad como la de los pilotos.

Gary Johnson, Kates Cottage

Racing on the Isle of Man

Nowhere else packs so much motor sport into a such small area as the Isle of Man and none of the events held at this magic venue is as famous as the TT.

It is a uniquely challenging motorcycle race, pitting competitors against an extraordinarily long and hazardous high-speed circuit, on town and country roads in daily use.

The vast majority of TT races have effectively been time-trials, with riders starting at intervals. So placings are determined by elapsed time, rather than their position on the road relative to other riders. It is not unknown for the first rider crossing the finish line to find that they have not won, since a rider finishing later has completed the race in a shorter time.

Such a long circuit takes time to learn and another feature of the TT is a prolonged period of practice and qualifying. Even experienced riders need track time to sort their machinery and work up to race pace. In the old days all practising took place just after dawn, but nowadays there are six evening sessions preceding the first race and three additional sessions slotted in on race days.

The TT's origins date back to the infancy of motorsport in the early 20th century. Racing on roads was banned in Britain, but the Isle of Man government, which can make its own laws, was persuaded to pass legislation allowing roads to be temporarily closed for the purpose. Car racers were the first to take advantage in 1904 and the first all-motorcycle Tourist Trophy race was staged three years later. As the name suggests, the event was for standard production motorcycles, with the aim of stimulating development through competition. The first races were over a 15.8mile (25.45km) circuit based at the village of St John's.

The legendary Mountain Course was

adopted for two-wheelers from 1911, when its gruelling climb through the hills demanded that makers enter more powerful machines with improved transmissions. The Senior race was dominated by American-made Indian motorcycles, a wake-up call for British factories.

The First World War caused a five-year hiatus, but TT racing returned in 1920 on the Mountain Course in use today, nominally 37.73 miles (60.72km) in length. Motorcycle evolution moved rapidly and the TT became a hotbed of technical development, as engineers sought the speed and reliability needed for TT success. The first 70mph (112.7km/h) lap of the Course was achieved in 1926 and the 80mph (128.7km/h) barrier was broken five years later.

By the 1930s, ever higher speeds were making the TT one of the most spectacular shows on earth and an elite of superstars gained a fan following. They included the shrewd yet genial Irishman Stanley Woods, gritty Scot Jimmy Guthrie, Lincolnshire tough guy Freddie Frith and Jimmy Simpson, who broke the lap record five times, yet only won once. British makes like Excelsior, Norton, Rudge and Velocette did most of the winning, but Moto Guzzi and Benelli of Italy along with BMW and DKW of Germany also took TT victories.

When World War Two stopped racing for seven years, Harold Daniell held the outright lap record at 91mph. Although his factory 500cc Norton was in a different class from showroom machines of the day, it is worth reflecting that Daniell was riding a narrower, twistier and bumpier course than today's and crude suspension with skinny tyres.

Racing resumed in 1947, when the Island was enjoying a tourist boom. Low-grade petrol held speeds down at first, but in 1950 rising young star Geoff Duke raised the record to 93.53mph on a Norton with a superbly stable new frame, nicknamed the 'featherbed'.

When the FIM road racing world championships began in 1949 this was the most challenging round, where more than 20 European manufacturers would contend for honours. Italy ruled: Benelli, Gilera, Mondial, Moto Guzzi and MV Agusta scooped 26 wins across all the solo classes in the 1950s. The Golden Jubilee TT of 1957 saw the eagerly-awaited first 100mph laps, set by fearless Scot Bob McIntyre on a Gilera in the Senior race, run over eight laps (302m/486km) on that one occasion only.

It wasn't realised at the time, but the appearance in 1959 of small 125cc bikes from the little-known Honda company heralded a new age of Japanese domination. By the mid-1960s, the Island's hills echoed to the open exhausts of engines with anything up to six cylinders as Honda battled with Yamaha and Suzuki for supremacy. Mike Hailwood gave Japan its first Senior trophy, winning on a Honda in 1966.

'Mike the Bike' was the brightest of a galaxy of grand prix stars at the TT in the 1960s, winning 12 races between 1961 and 1967. Other world champions shining on the island in that decade were Bill Ivy, Gary Hocking, Giacomo Agostini, Hugh Anderson, Jim Redman, Luigi Taveri, Phil Read, plus Sidecar heroes Fritz Scheidegger, Helmut Fath and Max Deubel.

A titanic battle in the six-lap 1967 Senior between Hailwood (Honda) and Agostini (MV) was one of the most thrilling races in TT history. Both riders lapped at a record-smashing 108mph until the Italian rider's drive chain broke on the fifth of six laps.

Honda withdrew its GP team at the end of 1967 and Hailwood retired. With less opposition, 'Ago' collected nine wins to make his total 10. Yamaha kept its team going another year and in 1968, factory rider Ivy dramatically set the first 100mph lap by a 125cc machine, on his four-cylinder 125cc two-stroke. From 1969 new GP rules restricted the number of cylinders and gear ratios in each capacity class.

Stanley Woods & Mike Hailwood, 1980 TT

Joey Dunlop, 2000 F1 TT

Although the TT grew to be one of the world's great motorcycling festivals in the 1970s, the races faced crisis. As one of the last of the old-style road circuits left on the GP calendar, the Mountain Course and its exceptional dangers attracted mounting criticism. When newcomer Gilberto Parlotti died after crashing on a wet road in 1972, Agostini boycotted the TT again and several other top GP riders joined him. The TT's grand prix status was withdrawn by the FIM after 1976 but a new format, including FIM-sanctioned TT championships for Formula 1, 2 and 3 production-based motorcycles, set the event on the road to recovery. With much more money to be won, several top British and Irish riders elected to become TT specialists.

In 1978 a sensational Hailwood come-back attracted record crowds, who revelled in the returning hero's Ducati-mounted TT Formula 1 win over previous TT refusenik Phil Read (Honda), who had come back to the Island in 1977 to win the first F1 race.

With racing for large capacity four-strokes growing in popularity and importance to manufacturers, the Formula 1 race had a long life. Last run in 2004, it was superseded by the broadly similar Superbike event. Seven Formula 1 races from 1983 to 2000 were won, six consecutively, by the ultimate TT legend Joey Dunlop. The quiet Ulsterman, with Honda for most of his long TT career, endeared himself to fans with his supreme skill, generous spirit and total lack of swagger. Another fans' favourite was likeable Scot Steve Hislop, who set out to be a master of the Mountain and succeeded, achieving the first official 120mph lap in the 1989 F1 race on a 750cc Honda. Sadly, both died in accidents, but not on the Island.

A Foot and Mouth disease epidemic on UK farms caused the 2001 races to be cancelled, interrupting a scintillating run of success by the phenomenal and popular David Jefferies. He took three wins in 1999 on Yamaha, and in 2000 when he set the first 125mph lap, then again in 2002 on Suzuki. The tragedy of David's death in a 2003 practice crash cast a shadow over that year's TT.

Not for the first time, the future of the races looked uncertain. But the Isle of Man government and the ACU authority for the sport in the UK saved the day, helped by well-attended celebrations of two centenaries, of the TT itself in 2007 and that of the Mountain Course in 2011. No riders are pressured into taking part, but those who relish riding on the Mountain Course are made welcome and TT talent scouts attend other 'real roads' events. Off-the-pace 'holiday racers' have been eliminated and today's TT riders are highly respected in the world of motor sport. Excellent TV coverage has helped stoke up worldwide interest in the TT.

The latest line-up of TT superheroes includes John McGuinness, with 20 wins notched up between 1999 and 2013, Michael Dunlop of the incredible Dunlop dynasty and TV personality Guy Martin. Rising stars to watch are James Hillier and Josh Brookes. In recent years, machinery from Japan's manufacturing giants has dominated, although the enlightened 'zero emissions' race for electrically-powered prototypes staged since 2009 has seen American technology take the lead.

Successfully introduced in 2013, the Isle of Man Festival of Motorcycling evolved out of the traditional late-summer Manx Grand Prix meeting for club riders and those seeking pre-TT experience. Dating from 1930, the Manx GP replaced the Amateur TT of 1923 to 1929 and included races for machines conforming to historic racing formulae from the 1980s.

The highlight of the August festival is the Classic TT racing, attracting an international entry with top TT stars encouraged to ride period and replica classics along with regular historic competitors, while Manx GP races continue as a nursery for budding TT riders and amateur racers. Other festival attractions include a day of speed and noise at Jurby, the island's short circuit on a former airfield in the north of the Island, plus the tough Manx Two-Day trial taking in some of the Island's remotest and most scenic places and there's a Manx Classic trial, too.

The last car races were held from 1947 to 1953 on a 3.8mile circuit based at the TT grandstand. However, since the 1960s the Island has hosted Britain's most challenging car rallies.

Although not as world-famous as the TT, the Southern 100 motorcycle meeting held on the Billown circuit over four weekdays in July is a friendly, action-packed event that shouldn't be missed. First staged in 1955, when the premier race for 500cc was over 100 miles, the meeting includes atmospheric evening races. Past solo winners include top TT riders, including Bob McIntyre, Charlie Williams and four members of the Dunlop family. The late Joey Dunlop won no less than 42 races at the Southern 100.

Not unlike some Irish race meetings, the Southern combines the difficulty and danger of public roads racing with the hectic wheel-to-wheel dicing created by massed starts. The 4.25-mile (6.44km) circuit is roughly square shaped with four sharp right-turns, a long downhill straight, plus numerous twists, turns and crests. As with the Mountain Course hazards include kerbs, stone walls and telephone poles, only these roads are narrower. The start, finish and paddock area is on the

TT TOP TEN	
Riders with the most wins	
26 Joey Dunlop	(1977-2000)
20 John McGuinness	(1999 –2013)
16 Dave Molyneux, Sidecar	(1989 – 2012)
14 Mike Hailwood	(1961-1979)
11 Phillip McCallen	(1992-1997)
11 Steve Hislop	(1987-1994)
10 Giacomo Agostini	(1966-1972)
10 Ian Lougher	(1997-2009)
10 Rob Fisher, Sidecar	(1994-2002)
10 Stanley Woods	(1923-1939)

outskirts of historic Castletown. Two other great meetings are hosted at Billown at TT time: the Pre TT Classic Road Races and Post TT Road Races.

Sidecars

Sidecar races add diversity and spectacle to the TT. Far removed from the traditional motorcycle and sidecar combination for road use, racing outfits are technically sophisticated, if lopsided, speed projectiles.

Drivers aim them heroically between hedges and kerbs, while passengers hang on tight, shifting their weight to aid stability at speeds up to 135mph. Spectators love it, especially on the twistier or bumpier parts of the course.

First staged from 1923 to 1925, the Sidecar TT was re-introduced on the 10.79-mile Clypse Circuit used for some classes from 1954 to 1959, then returned permanently to the Mountain Course from 1960. Under the current formula engines have to be of a production type of up to 600cc.

Current TT solo classes

Superbike: machines conforming to an international Superbike formula. Twin-cylinder engines up to 1200c, three- or four-cylinder engines up to 1000cc

Superstock: conforming production models with capacity limits as for Superbike

Supersport: conforming production machines with approved modifications. Capacity limits: twins up to 750cc, triples 675cc and fours 600cc.

Lightweight production-based machines with twin-cylinder engines up to 650cc

Senior TT for Superbike, Supersport and Superstock, plus approved pure racing or prototype machines.

Zero TT: prototype electric motorcycles (one lap only)

There are three Classic TT races: for machines up to 350cc, up to 500cc and a combined event for machines conforming to Formula 1 Classic and Formula 2 Classic categories.

Roy Hanks/Kevin Perry, Cronk-y-Voddy, TT

Rennen auf der Isle of Man

Nirgends findet man auf so kleinem Gebiet so viel Motorsport wie auf der Isle of Man. Und keine der Veranstaltungen an diesem sagenhaften Ort ist so berühmt wie die TT.

Hierbei handelt es sich um ein besonders anspruchsvolles Motorradrennen, bei dem die Kontrahenten auf einer außergewöhnlich langen und gefährlichen Hochgeschwindigkeitsstrecke gegeneinander antreten, die durch Städte und über Landstraßen führt, die täglich befahren werden.

Bei den meisten TT-Rennen handelt es sich tatsächlich um Zeitfahrten, bei denen die Fahrer zeitversetzt starten. Die Platzierungen werden somit anhand der erzielten Zeit und nicht durch die Position auf der Strecke in Bezug zu den anderen Fahrern ermittelt. Es kann deshalb durchaus vorkommen, dass der Fahrer, der die Ziellinie zuerst überquert, gar nicht der Sieger ist, weil ein anderer Fahrer, der später ins Ziel kommt, die Strecke in kürzerer Zeit bewältigt hat.

Eine so lange Rennstrecke erfordert viel Übung, deshalb sind ausgiebige Trainings und Qualifyings ein weiteres Merkmal der TT. Selbst erfahrene Fahrer müssen viel Zeit auf der Strecke verbringen, um ihre Maschine korrekt anzupassen und sich für das Rennen fit zu machen. Früher fanden alle Übungen kurz nach Sonnenaufgang statt. Heutzutage gibt es sechs Abendübungen vor dem ersten Rennen und drei zusätzliche Übungen an den Renntagen.

Die TT nahm ihren Anfang, als der Motorsport zu Beginn des 20. Jahrhunderts noch in den Kinderschuhen steckte. In Großbritannien wurden Rennen auf öffentlichen Straßen verboten, doch die Regierung der Isle of Man, die eigene Gesetze verabschieden kann, erließ eine Verordnung, die es gestattete, Straßen für die Durchführung von Rennen vorübergehend zu sperren. Diese wurde 1904 zuerst für Autorennen genutzt. Drei Jahre später wurde das erste Rennen nur für Motorräder – die Tourist Trophy – veranstaltet. Das Rennen war für serienmäßig produzierte Motorräder ausgelegt und sollte durch den Wettbewerb die Entwicklung der Maschinen ankurbeln. Die ersten Rennen fanden auf der 25,45 km langen Strecke in der Nähe des Dorfes St John's statt.

Ab 1911 führten die Rennen für Zweiräder über den legendären Snaefell Mountain Course. Der aufreibende Anstieg auf der Bergstrecke zwang die Hersteller, leistungsstärkere Maschinen mit besserem Getriebe an den Start gehen zu lassen. Die Rennen der Senior-Klasse wurden von den in Amerika hergestellten Indian-Motorrädern dominiert. Dies war ein Weckruf für britische Hersteller.

Durch den Ersten Weltkrieg fiel das TT-Rennen fünf Jahre lang aus und wurde 1920 wieder auf der noch heute verwendeten 60,72 km langen Bergstrecke wieder aufgenommen. Die Motorräder wurden schnell weiterentwickelt und die TT wurde zu einer Keimzelle technischer Entwicklung, da die Ingenieure versuchten, durch Geschwindigkeit und Zuverlässigkeit der Maschinen den Erfolg zu erringen. 1926 wurde die Strecke zum ersten Mal mit einer Geschwindigkeit von 112,7 km/h absolviert und fünf Jahre später wurde mit 128,7 km/h ein neuer Rekord aufgestellt.

In den 1930ern wurde das TT-Rennen durch noch höhere Geschwindigkeiten eines der eindrucksvollsten Spektakel der Welt und einige herausragende Superstars eroberten eine eigene Fangemeinde. Dazu gehörten der gewitzte und freundliche Ire Stanley Woods, der mutige Schotte Jimmy Guthrie, Freddie Frith, ein harter Kerl aus Lincolnshire, und Jimmy Simpson, der fünf Mal den Rundenrekord aufstellte, aber nur einmal das Rennen gewann. Meist waren britische Marken, wie Excelsior, Norton, Rudge und Velocette die Motorräder der Sieger. Aber auch die italienischen Marken Moto Guzzi und Benelli sowie BMW und DKW aus Deutschland triumphierten im TT-Rennen.

Als der Zweite Weltkrieg das Rennen sieben Jahre lang unterbrach, hatte Harold Daniell den kompletten Rundenrekord mit 146,5 km/h inne. Zwar befand sich seine werksgefertigte Norton mit einem Hubraum von 500 cm_ in einer anderen Klasse als die damals speziell angefertigten Maschinen, aber man muss beachten, dass die Strecke zu Daniells Zeit schmaler, kurvenreicher und unebener als heute war und dass er nur über eine einfache Aufhängung und schmale Reifen verfügte.

Im Jahr 1947 wurden die Rennen wieder aufgenommen und die Insel erlebte einen Tourismus-Boom. Minderwertiges Benzin drückte zunächst die Geschwindigkeit, aber 1950 konnte der junge aufstrebende Star Geoff Duke einen neuen Rekord über 150,5 km/h auf einer Norton mit einem herausragend stabilen neuen Rahmen mit dem Spitznamen „Featherbed" (Federbett) aufstellen.

Als 1949 die Motorradweltmeisterschaft der FIM begann, war die TT die schwierigste Runde und über 20 europäische Hersteller wetteiferten um den Sieg. Italien lag klar in Führung: Benelli, Gilera, Mondial, Moto Guzzi und MV Agusta fuhren in den 1950ern 26 Siege in allen Soloklassen ein. Als die TT 1957 ihren fünfzigsten Geburtstag feierte, brach der furchtlose Schotte Bob McIntyre zum ersten Mal die 100mph-Marke (160,9 km/h). Er fuhr eine Gilera in einem Rennen der Senior-Klasse über acht Runden (486 km).

Es war damals niemandem bewusst, doch als 1959 zum ersten Mal kleine 125-cm_-Maschinen des kaum bekannten Herstellers Honda am Rennen teil nahmen, läutete dies eine neue Zeit japanischer Überlegenheit ein. Mitte der 1960er Jahre hallten die Berge von den Motoren mit bis zu sechs Zylindern wider, als Honda mit Yamaha und Suzuki um die Vorherrschaft kämpfte. Mike Hailwood gewann 1966 mit einer Honda zum ersten Mal die Senior-Klasse für Japan.

„Mike the Bike" war in den 1960ern der strahlendste Stern in einer Galaxie aus TT-Rennstars und gewann zwischen 1961 und 1967 zwölf Rennen. Andere Weltmeister, die sich in diesem Jahrzehnt auf der Insel hervortaten, waren Bill Ivy, Gary Hocking, Giacomo Agostini, Hugh Anderson, Jim Redman, Luigi Taveri, Phil Read sowie die Gespannhelden Fritz Scheidegger, Helmut Fath und Max Deubel.

Ein Kampf der Titanen zwischen Hailwood (Honda) und Agostini (MV) machte 1967 das Rennen der Senior-Klasse über sechs Runden zu einem der spannendsten Wettkämpfe in der Geschichte der TT. Beide Fahrer legten eine Rekordgeschwindigkeit von 173,8 km/h auf den Asphalt, bis in der fünften von sechs Runden die Antriebskette des Italieners riss.

Ende 1967 zog Honda sein GP-Team zurück und Hailwood beendete seine Karriere. Mit weniger Konkurrenz fuhr „Ago" noch neun Siege ein und kam so auf eine Gesamtbilanz von 10 Siegen. Yamaha nahm noch

Giacomo Agostini/John McGuinness, Classic TT

ein weiteres Jahr teil und 1968 erzielte zum ersten Mal eine 125-cm_-Maschine eine Geschwindigkeit von 100 mph (160,9 km/h). Der Yamaha-Fahrer Bill Ivy erlangte diesen Erfolg mit seiner Vierzylinder-Zweitaktmaschine. Ab 1969 beschränkten neue Rennregeln die Anzahl zulässiger Zylinder in allen Klassen.

Obwohl die TT in den 1970ern zu einem der größten Motorsportfestivals der Welt heranwuchs, geriet das Rennen in eine Krise. Die Bergstrecke war eine der letzten Strecken des GP im alten Stil und mit erheblichen Gefahren verbunden. Dadurch nahm die Kritik an ihr zu. Als der Neueinsteiger Gilberto Parlotti 1972 bei einem Unfall auf der nassen Straße starb, boykottierte Agostini erneut die TT und einige andere Spitzenfahrer taten es ihm gleich. Der TT wurde nach 1976 von der FIM der Weltmeisterschaftsstatus entzogen. Doch ein neues Format mit von der FIM genehmigten TT-Meisterschaften für Motorräder, die für die Formula 1, 2 und 3 hergestellt wurden, brachte die Veranstaltung auf einen neuen Weg. Da es viel mehr Geld zu gewinnen gab, wurden einige der besten britischen und irischen Fahrer zu TT-Spezialisten.

1978 brach das sensationelle Comeback Hailwoods alle Zuschauerrekorde. Die Fans freuten sich über den

Sieg in der TT Formula 1 des zurückgekehrten Helden mit seiner Ducati über den ehemaligen TT-Boykottierer Phil Read (Honda), der 1977 auf die Insel zurückgekehrt war und das erste F1-Rennen gewonnen hatte.

Die Rennen für Motorräder mit großem Hubraum gewannen zunehmend an Beliebtheit und wurden so für die Hersteller immer wichtiger, was der Formula 1 ein langes Leben bescherte. Zum letzten Mal wurde sie 2004 ausgetragen und dann durch das weitgehend gleiche Superbike-Rennen abgelöst. Die größte TT-Legende Joey Dunlop gewann von 1983 bis 2000 sieben Formula-1-Rennen, sechs davon in Folge. Der zurückhaltende Nordire, der den größten Teil seiner langen TT-Karriere auf einer Honda verbrachte, gewann durch seine überlegenen Fähigkeiten, Großzügigkeit und Bescheidenheit die Herzen der Fans. Ein weiterer Liebling der Fans war der sympathische Schotte Steve Hislop, der 1989 zum ersten Mal offiziell die 120-mph-Barriere (193,1 km/h) in einem F1 Rennen mit einer 750-cm3-Honda bezwang. Leider verunglückten später beide Rennfahrer, jedoch nicht auf der Isle of Man.

Aufgrund der Maul- und Klauenseuche, die in britischen Viehbetrieben ausgebrochen war, mussten die Rennen 2001 abgesagt werden. Dies unterbrach die

Steve Hislop, TT

Michael Dunlop, John McGuinness, Bruce Anstey, Senior TT 2013

strahlende Erfolgsserie des überragenden und beliebten David Jefferies. Er gewann drei Mal in den Jahren 1999 und 2000, als er zum ersten Mal eine Geschwindigkeit von 201 km/h erreichte. Diese Siege errang er auf einer Yamaha. 2002 war er auf einer Suzuki erneut siegreich. Davids tragischer Tod im Jahr 2003 bei einem Trainingsunfall überschattete die TT dieses Jahres.

Nicht zum ersten Mal schien die Zukunft der Rennen ungewiss. Aber die Regierung der Isle of Man und die britische Motorradsportbehörde ACU konnten die Veranstaltung retten, wozu auch zwei gut besuchte Jahrhundertfeiern beitrugen: der 100. Geburtstag der TT im Jahr 2007 sowie der Bergstrecke im Jahr 2011. Die Fahrer werden nicht zur Teilnahme gedrängt, doch diejenigen, die auf der Bergstrecke fahren möchten, sind herzlich willkommen. Außerdem besuchen TT-Talentsucher auch andere Straßenrennen. „Sonntagsrennfahrern" ist die Teilnahme nicht länger gestattet und heute sind TT-Fahrer in der Welt des Motorsports hoch angesehen. Durch die ausgezeichnete TV-Berichterstattung wurde weltweit das Interesse an der TT geschürt.

Zu den aktuellen Helden der TT gehören John McGuinness, der 20 Siege zwischen 1999 und 2013 errungen hat, Michael Dunlop aus der unvergleichlichen

Dunlop-Familie und der Fernsehstar Guy Martin. Aufstrebende Stars, die man im Auge behalten sollte, sind James Hillier und Josh Brookes. In den vergangenen Jahren lagen Maschinen großer japanischer Hersteller an der Spitze. Doch im visionären „Zero Emissions Race" für elektrisch angetriebene Prototypen, das seit 2009 stattfindet, hat amerikanische Technik die Nase vorn.

Das 2013 eingeführte Isle of Man Festival of Motorcycling entwickelte sich aus dem traditionellen Manx Grand Prix, bei dem sich im Spätsommer Amateurfahrer und Fahrer trafen, die vor einer TT-Teilnahme Erfahrungen sammeln wollten. Seit 1930 ersetzte der Manx GP die Amateur TT von 1923-1929. Er beinhaltete auch Rennen für Maschinen, die den Anforderungen historischer Rennen aus den 1980ern entsprachen.

Der Höhepunkt des im August stattfindenden Festivals ist das Classic-TT-Rennen, das internationale Teilnehmer einschließlich TT-Topstars anzieht, die mit originalen und nachgebauten Oldtimern gegen langjährige Teilnehmer antreten. Die Manx-GP-Rennen sind zudem ein Anlaufpunkt für angehende TT-Fahrer und Amateure. Weitere Attraktionen des Festivals sind ein Tag voll Geschwindigkeit und Lärm auf Jurby, einer Kurzstrecke auf einem ehemaligen Flugplatz im Norden der Insel, sowie das harte Manx Two Day Trial an einigen der schönsten und entlegensten Orte der Insel, es gibt außerdem auch ein Trial für Oldtimer.

Die letzten Autorennen fanden von 1947-1953 auf einer 6,1 km langen Strecke an der TT-Haupttribüne statt. Seit den 1960ern ist die Insel jedoch der Austragungsort der schwierigsten britischen Auto-Rallyes.

Wenn auch nicht so bekannt wie die TT, ist das Southern-100-Motorradtreffen, das an vier Wochentagen im Juli auf der Billown-Strecke veranstaltet wird, ein freundliches, ereignisreiches Event, das man nicht verpassen sollte. Es fand zum ersten Mal 1955 statt. Damals war das Rennen der Königsklasse für Maschinen mit 500 cm_ Hubraum über 160 km lang. Zu dem Treffen gehören auch stimmungsvolle Abendrennen. Zu den ehemaligen Solosiegern gehören hochrangige TT-Fahrer, wie Bob McIntyre, Charlie Williams und vier Mitglieder der Dunlop-Familie. Der verstorbene Joey Dunlop gewann nicht weniger als 42 Rennen des Southern 100.

Ähnlich wie manche irischen Rennen vereint das Southern 100 die Schwierigkeiten und Gefahren eines Straßenrennens mit den aufregenden Rad-an-Rad-Duellen, die durch Massenstarts entstehen. Die 6,44 km lange Strecke hat grob die Form eines Rechtecks mit vier engen Rechtskurven, einer langen bergab führenden Gerade und zahlreiche Biegungen und Hügel. Wie bei der Bergstrecke stellen Bordsteine, Steinmauern und Telefonmasten einige der Gefahren dar. Allerdings sind hier die Straßen schmaler. Start, Ziel und Fahrerlager befinden sich am Rand von Castletown. Zur selben Zeit wie die TT werden in Billown noch zwei weitere große

Treffen veranstaltet: die Pre TT Classic Road Races und die Post TT Road Races.

Motorradgespanne

Motorradgespanne bereichern die TT und machen sie abwechslungsreicher. In Rennen eingesetzte Motorradgespanne haben wenig mit den Motorrädern und Beiwagen zu tun, die im normalen Straßenverkehr eingesetzt werden. Sie sind technisch ausgereifte, deutlich zur Seite neigende Geschosse.

Die Fahrer wagen sich heldenhaft zwischen Hecken und Bordsteinen hindurch, während sich die Beifahrer gut festhalten und durch Gewichtsverlagerung die Stabilität erhöhen, was bei Geschwindigkeiten bis zu 217 km/h auch nötig ist. Die Zuschauer sind begeistert, besonders bei den kurvigen oder holprigen Streckenabschnitten.

Die Sidecar TT fand zum ersten Mal von 1923 bis 1925 statt und wurde von 1945 bis 1959 für einige Klassen auf der 17,36 km langen Clypse-Strecke wiedereingeführt. Seit 1960 findet das Rennen auf der Bergstrecke statt. Gemäß den aktuellen Regeln dürfen die Motoren einen Hubraum von bis zu 600 cm3 haben.

Aktuelle TT-Soloklassen

Superbike: Maschinen, die den internationalen Regeln für Superbikes entsprechen. Zweizylindermotoren mit bis zu 1200cm3 Hubraum, Drei- oder Vierzylindermotoren mit bis zu 1000cm3 Hubraum.

Superstock: regelgerechte Serienmodelle mit denselben Hubraumbeschränkungen wie Superbikes.

Supersport: regelgerechte Serienmodelle mit genehmigten Modifikationen. Hubraumbeschränkungen: Zweizylinder bis 750cm3, Dreizylinder bis 675cm3, Vierzylinder bis 600cm3.

Leichte, seriengefertigte Maschinen mit Zweizylindermotoren bis 650cm3.

Senior TT für Superbike, Supersport und Superstock sowie genehmigte Rennmaschinen und Prototypen.

Zero TT: Prototypen von Elektromotorrädern (nur eine Runde).

Es gibt drei Classic-TT-Rennen: für Maschinen bis 350cm3 und bis 500cm3 sowie eine Kombination für Maschinen, die den Kategorien Formula 1 Classic und Formula 2 Classic entsprechen.

DIE ZEHN TT-FAHRER MIT DEN MEISTEN SIEGEN:	
26 Joey Dunlop	(1977-2000)
20 John McGuinness	(1999 –2013)
16 Dave Molyneux, Sidecar	(1989 – 2012)
14 Mike Hailwood	(1961-1979)
11 Phillip McCallen	(1992-1997)
11 Steve Hislop	(1987-1994)
10 Giacomo Agostini	(1966-1972)
10 Ian Lougher	(1997-2009)
10 Rob Fisher, Sidecar	(1994-2002)
10 Stanley Woods	(1923-1939)

Racing sur l'Île de Man

Nulle part ailleurs se produisent autant d'évènements de sport automobile sur une surface si petite que celle de l'Île de Man qui accueille le célèbre TT.

C'est une course de moto disputée unique, opposant des concurrents sur un circuit à grande vitesse extraordinairement long et dangereux, se déroulant sur des routes urbaines et rurales empruntées quotidiennement.

La grande majorité des courses TT sont effectivement des courses contre la montre où les pilotes partent par intervalles. Les classements sont établis par le temps écoulé, plutôt que selon la position sur la route par rapport aux autres participants. Il n'est pas rare que le premier pilote apprenne en franchissant la ligne d'arrivée que le gagnant définitif sera celui qui aura terminé la course en moins de temps.

Il faut du temps avant de maîtriser ce type de long circuit et le TT se caractérise également par une longue période d'entraînement et de qualification. Même les pilotes expérimentés ont besoin de passer du temps sur la piste de manière à mettre au point leur machine et à se mettre dans le rythme de la course. Jadis, toutes les activités commençaient à l'aube, aujourd'hui il existe six sessions diurnes précédant la première course et trois sessions supplémentaires organisées pendant les jours de course.

Le TT remonte aux balbutiements du sport automobile au début du 20 ème siècle. Les courses sur routes étaient interdites en Grande-Bretagne, mais le gouvernement auto-législateur de l'Île de Man parvint à faire adopter une loi prévoyant la fermeture temporaire des routes à ces occasions. Les conducteurs automobiles furent les premiers à en bénéficier en 1904 et la première course de moto Tourist Trophy eut lieu trois ans plus tard. Ainsi que son nom l'indique, l'évènement était destiné aux motos de fabrication standard, dans le but de stimuler le développement par la compétition. Les

premières courses se disputaient sur un circuit de 15,8 miles (25,45 km) basé dans le village de St John's.

La légendaire Montain Course accordée aux deux roues remonte à 1911. Son ascension à travers les collines étant si éprouvante, il fut demandé aux décideurs de faire entrer des machines plus puissantes dotées d'une transmission améliorée. La course senior fut dominée par Indian motorcycles de fabrication américaine, un signal d'alarme pour les usines britanniques.

Le TT fut interrompu pendant cinq ans suite à la Première guerre mondiale, puis fit son grand retour en 1920 avec sa course de montagne encore disputée aujourd'hui, théoriquement de 37,73 miles (60,72 km) de long. L'évolution du monde de la moto s'accéléra et le TT devint une pépinière de progrès techniques sous l'égide d'ingénieurs qui recherchaient la rapidité et la fiabilité nécessaire au succès du TT. Le premier tour de course à 70 mph (112,7 km/h) fut atteint en 1926 et une pointe à 80 mph (128,7 km/h) fut franchie cinq ans plus tard.

Dans les années 1930, des vitesses toujours plus soutenues firent du TT un des évènements le plus spectaculaire au monde attirant une foule immense de fans de superstars. Mentionnons notamment le perspicace Irlandais de génie Stanley Woods, le courageux Scot Jimmy Guthrie, les durs à cuir du Lincolnshire Freddie Frith et Jimmy Simpson qui battirent cinq fois le record du tour pourtant remporté qu'une seule fois. Les marques britanniques telles que Excelsior, Norton, Rudge et Velocette furent les grandes gagnantes. Toutefois, Moto Guzzi et Benelli d'Italie ainsi que BMW et DKW d'Allemagne décrochèrent également des victoires au TT.

Le TT fut interrompu pendant sept ans suite à la Seconde guerre mondiale, Harold Daniell détint le record du tour absolu à 91 mph. Malgré sa 500 cm3, Norton se trouvait dans une classe différente de celle des machines de salles d'exposition d'aujourd'hui. Il convient de souligner que les circuits parcourus par Daniell étaient plus étroits, sinueux et accidentés que ceux de maintenant et la suspension était rudimentaire et les pneus étroits.

Les courses reprirent en 1947, alors que l'île connaissait un essor touristique. Au début, l'essence de mauvaise qualité limita la vitesse, mais en 1950, la toute nouvelle star de la moto, Geoff Duke, dépassa les 93,53 mph sur une Norton dotée d'un nouveau cadre parfaitement stable appelé le « lit de plumes ».

Le championnat du monde FIM de course sur route débuta en 1949, ce fut le tour le plus disputé avec plus de 20 constructeurs européens représentés rivalisant pour l'honneur. L'Italie, la grande gagnante : Dans les années 50, Benelli, Gilera, Mondial, Moto Guzzi et MV Agusta remportèrent 26 victoires toutes catégories en solitaire confondues. Lors du Golden Jubilee TT de 1957, l'intrépide Scot Bob McIntyre atteignit, à cette occasion uniquement, le record tant attendu de tours à 100 mph sur une Gilera dans la course Senior sur un parcours de huit tours (302 miles/486 km).

Ce ne fut pas le cas cette année, mais lorsque les petites motos de 125 cm3 de l'entreprise Honda encore peu connue firent leur entrée en 1959, une nouvelle ère de domination japonaise s'annonça. Au milieu des années 1960, les collines de l'île firent l'écho aux systèmes d'échappement ouverts des moteurs jusqu'à six cylindres comme ceux de Honda livrant bataille contre Yamaha et Suzuki pour la suprématie. Le Japon gagna en 1966 son premier Senior trophy avec Mike Hailwood, grand gagnant sur une Honda.

« Mike the Bike » fut la véritable star des stars de la pléiade des grands prix de TT dans les années 1960 en remportant pas moins de 12 courses entre 1961 et 1967. D'autres champions ont brillé sur l'île au cours de cette décennie tels que Bill Ivy, Gary Hocking, Giacomo Agostini, Hugh Anderson, Jim Redman, Luigi Taveri, Phil Read, sans compter les héros de side-car Fritz Scheidegger, Helmut Fath et Max Deubel.

On retiendra également la bataille titanesque sur les six tours Senior de 1967 que se livrèrent Hailwood (sur Honda) et Agostini (sur MV). Elle fut considérée comme étant l'une des courses la plus passionnante de l'histoire du TT. Les deux pilotes firent la course

Jimmy Guthrie

en brisant le record avec une vitesse de tour de 108 mph avant que la chaîne d'entraînement du pilote italien ne se brise au cinquième tour sur six.

Honda quitta son équipe de GP à la fin 1967 et Hailwood se retira. Avec moins d'adversaires, « Ago » remporta neufs victoires pour arriver à un total de dix. Yamaha garda son équipe encore un an et, en 1968, le pilote d'usine Ivy atteignit pour la première fois les 100 mph sur une machine de 125 cm3, sa 125 cm3 équipée d'un moteur quatre cylindres à deux temps. À partir de 1969, le nouveau règlement du GP limita le nombre de cylindres et de rapports dans chaque classe de puissance.

Bien que le TT soit devenu un des plus grands festivals de moto au monde dans les années 1970, les courses connurent la crise. La Montain Course aux dangers exceptionnels dénoncés par la critique grandissante se veut être un des derniers circuits sur route à l'ancienne sur le calendrier du GP. Lorsque le nouveau venu, Gilberto Parlotti, décéda en 1972 des suites d'un dérapage sur une chaussée mouillée, Agostini boycotta le TT et plusieurs autres pilotes stars du GP le rejoignirent. Le statut de grand prix du TT fut retiré par la FIM après 1976, mais un nouveau modèle d'évaluation, incluant les championnats TT sanctionnés par la FIM, basé sur la production de motos destinées à la Formula 1, 2 et 3, amorça une relance économique. Avec plus d'argent à gagner, plusieurs pilotes britanniques et irlandais choisirent de devenir des spécialistes TT.

En 1978, Hailwood fit un retour exceptionnel attirant un record de foule, il se délecta de sa victoire au TT Formula 1 sur Ducati comme son prédécesseur le refusenik de TT, Phil Read (Honda) qui fit son retour sur l'île en 1977 pour gagner la première course F1.

La Formula 1 eut une longue carrière avec un racing pour des moteurs à quatre temps de grande capacité au succès grandissant, prenant de l'importance pour les fabricants. La dernière course en 2004 fut remplacée par l'évènement Superbike similaire pour l'essentiel. Sept courses de Formula 1 de 1983 à 2000, dont six consécutives, furent gagnées par la légende du TT Joey Dunlop. Le calme Ulsterman, sur Honda la majeure partie de sa carrière, gagna l'affection des fans en raison de son talent absolu, sa générosité et son absence totale d'arrogance. Un autre préféré des fans, le sympathique Scot Steve Hislop qui s'avéra être le maître de la Mountain et réussit en 1989 à réaliser le premier tour officiel à 120 mph dans une course de F1 sur une Honda 750 cm3. Malheureusement, les deux décédèrent dans un accident mais pas sur l'île.

Les courses de 2001 furent annulées suite à l'épidémie de fièvre aphteuse qui toucha les fermes du Royaume-Uni, interrompant du même coup l'envolée vers le succès du phénoménal et populaire David Jefferies. Il remporta trois victoires en 1999 sur Yamaha, et en 2000 il signait le premier tour à 125 mph sur Yamaha, puis encore en 2002 mais sur

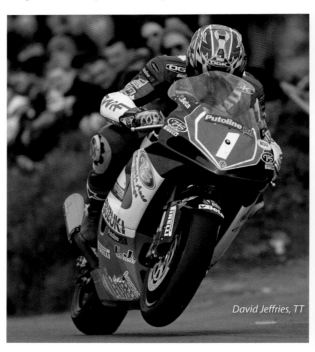

David Jefferies, TT

Suziki. La mort tragique de David survenue au cours d'un entraînement en 2003 jeta une ombre sur le TT de cette même année.

Une fois de plus, le futur des courses fut incertain. Mais le gouvernement de l'Île de Man et l'administration de l'Association of Commonwealth Universities (ACU) pour le sport au Royaume-Uni rétablirent la situation aidés par les festivités très suivies du bicentenaire du TT lui-même en 2007 et de celui de la Mountain Course en 2011. Aucun pilote n'est obligé de participer, mais ceux qui aiment parcourir la Mountain Course sont les bienvenus et les dénicheurs de talents TT participent à d'autres évènements sur « routes réelles ». Les « coureurs en villégiature » relégués ont été éliminés et les pilotes TT d'aujourd'hui sont très respectés dans le monde du sport automobile. Une excellente couverture télévisée permit d'attiser l'intérêt sur le TT à l'échelle mondiale.

Les derniers nés des super-héros s'appellent John McGuinness avec 20 victoires à son palmarès remportées entre 1999 et 2013, Michael Dunlop de l'incroyable dynastie Dunlop et la personnalité de télévision Guy Martin. Les étoiles montantes à voir sont James Hillier et Josh Brookes. Ces dernières années, les machines issues du géant de l'industrie japonaise ont dominée, bien que les courses à émission zéro avec des prototypes à moteur électrique mises en place depuis 2009 ont vu la technique américaine prendre la tête.

Lancé avec succès en 2013, le Festival de Moto de l'Île de Man né de la rencontre du Manx Grand Prix traditionnel de fin d'été est destiné aux coureurs en club et à ceux qui sont à la recherche d'une première expérience de TT. Datant de 1930, le Manx GP remplaça le TT amateur de 1923 et 1929 et rajouta des courses pour des machines répondant aux formules de courses historiques des années 1980.

La course Classic TT constitue le point phare du festival d'août, attirant un public international avec les stars du TT de haut niveau invitées à participer à des courses classiques de cette période et à des répliques avec des concurrents réguliers historiques, tandis que les courses du Manx GP permettent toujours l'émergence de pilotes TT et de coureurs amateurs. D'autres attractions du festival sont une journée de course à Jurby, le petit circuit de l'île sur

LES DIX PREMIERS PILOTES TT AYANT REMPORTÉ LE PLUS DE VICTOIRES	
26 Joey Dunlop	(1977-2000)
20 John McGuinness	(1999 –2013)
16 Dave Molyneux, Sidecar	(1989 – 2012)
14 Mike Hailwood	(1961-1979)
11 Phillip McCallen	(1992-1997)
11 Steve Hislop	(1987-1994)
10 Giacomo Agostini	(1966-1972)
10 Ian Lougher	(1997-2009)
10 Rob Fisher, Sidecar	(1994-2002)
10 Stanley Woods	(1923-1939)

l'ancien aérodrome au nord de l'île ainsi que le Manx Two-Day Trial assez dur ayant lieu dans plusieurs zones les plus reculées et pittoresques de l'île. Il y a aussi un Manx Classic Trial.

Les dernières courses de voiture furent organisées entre 1947 et 1953 sur un circuit de 3,8 miles basé sur le TT Grandstand. Néanmoins, depuis les années 60, l'île accueille les rallyes voiture britanniques les plus stimulants.

Bien que n'étant pas autant célèbre que le TT, le rendez-vous moto Southern 100 se déroule en juillet sur le circuit de Billown pendant quatre jours de la semaine et constitue un évènement amical bourré d'actions à ne pas manquer. Apparu en 1955, alors que la première course sur 500 cm3 se déroulait sur un circuit de plus de 100 miles, la rencontre offre des courses à l'atmosphère unique. Les anciens lauréats en solitaire dont les meilleurs pilotes sont Bob McIntyre, Charlie Williams et quatre membres de la famille Dunlop. Le dernier Joey Dunlop gagna pas moins de 42 courses au Southern 100.

Non loin de ressembler aux rencontres de courses irlandaises, le Southern réunit la difficulté et le danger sur des voies publiques avec la découpe effrénée roue contre roue due aux départs en groupe. Le circuit à peu près carré de 4,25 miles (6,44 km) avec quatre virages serrés à droite, une longue ligne droite descendante ainsi que de nombreux virages, courbes et crêtes. Il renferme des dangers similaires à la Mountain Course tels que des bordures de trottoirs, murets de pierre et poteaux téléphoniques, seules ces routes sont plus étroites. La zone de départ, d'arrivée et de paddock se trouve en périphérie de Castletown, capitale historique de l'Île de Man. Deux autres grandes rencontres se déroulent à Billown au moment du TT : les Pre TT Classic Road Races et les Post TT Road Races.

Side-cars

Les courses de side-car apportent diversité et spectacle au TT. Considérablement différentes des motos à side-car traditionnelles sur route, ils sont techniquement sophistiqués pouvant devenir de vrais bolides si asymétriques.

Les pilotes passent entre les haies et bordures de trottoirs avec héroïsme alors que les passagers se cramponnent fermement tout en déplaçant le poids de leur corps de manière à contribuer à la stabilité et cela à des vitesses dépassant les 135 mph. Les spectateurs adorent cela, notamment aux endroits les plus sinueux ou accidentés du circuit.

Apparu entre 1923 et 1925, le Sidecar TT fut réintroduit sur le Clypse Circuit de 10,79 miles utilisé pour certaines catégories entre 1954 et 1959 pour revenir définitivement à la Mountain Course à partir de 1960. La formula actuelle n'accepte que les moteurs ne dépassant pas les 600 cm3.

Catégories en solitaire TT actuelles

Superbike : machine répondant à la formula internationale de Superbike. Moteurs bicylindre jusqu'à 1200 cm3, moteurs à trois ou quatre cylindres jusqu'à 1000 cm3

Superstock : modèles de production conformes à puissance limitée comme pour le Superbike

Supersport : machines de production conformes avec modifications approuvées. Puissances limites : bicylindres jusqu'à 750 cm3, trois cylindres 675 cm3 et quatre cylindres 600 cm3

Machine légère dotée d'un moteur bicylindre jusqu'à 650 cm3

Senior TT pur Superbike, Supersport et Superstock ainsi que pur racing approuvé ou prototypes de machines.

Zero TT: prototypes de motos électriques (un tour uniquement)

Il existe trois courses Classic TT: une pour les machines jusqu'à 350 cm3, jusqu'à 500 cm3 et une pour une épreuve combinée pour machines conforme aux catégories de Formule 1 Classic et de Formule 2 Classic.

Gary Johnson, Keppel Gate, Classic TT

Zero TT: Motoczysz

Carreras en la Isla de Man

Ningún otro lugar en el mundo concentra tanto deporte del motor en tan poco espacio como las carreras de la Isla de Man, siendo el TT el evento más famoso de todos los celebrados en este mágico enclave.

Se trata de una prueba motociclista singularmente exigente en la que los pilotos han de enfrentarse a un circuito de alta velocidad extraordinariamente largo y arriesgado que discurre por vías urbanas y rurales de uso diario.

En la gran mayoría de las carreras del TT los pilotos salen a intervalos y se cronometran sus tiempos. Por tanto, la clasificación viene establecida por los tiempos conseguidos en lugar de la posición ocupada en relación con los demás pilotos. No es extraño que el primer piloto en cruzar la línea de meta no resulte ganador, dado que otro piloto que alcance la misma posteriormente puede haber completado el recorrido en menos tiempo.

Un circuito tan largo como este requiere tiempo para memorizarlo; otra de las características del TT son sus prolongadas sesiones de entrenamiento y calificación. Incluso los pilotos más experimentados necesitan rodar en el circuito para poner a punto sus máquinas y coger ritmo de carrera. Antiguamente todas las sesiones de entrenamiento se realizaban nada más amanecer, pero en la actualidad existen seis sesiones vespertinas previas a la primera carrera y otras tres intercaladas los días de competición.

Los orígenes del TT se remontan a comienzos del siglo XX, época en la que empiezan a dar sus primeros pasos los deportes de motor. En Gran Bretaña estaban prohibidas las carreras por las calles; sin embargo, se persuadió al gobierno de la Isla de Man, que podía dictar su propia legislación, para que promulgase una ley que permitiera cerrar temporalmente las calles al tráfico para disputar competiciones. Los primeros en sacar partido de esta legislación fueron los pilotos de coches (en 1904) y la primera carrera del Tourist Trophy únicamente con motos se disputó tres años más tarde. Como su nombre indica, la prueba estaba dirigida a motocicletas de serie estándar; se pretendía que la competición fuera la vía para mejorar la evolución de estas máquinas. Las primeras competiciones se celebraron en un circuito de 15,8 millas (25,45 km) en la localidad de St John's.

El legendario circuito de la montaña (Mountain Course) empezó a utilizarse para carreras de motos a partir de 1911; la dura ascensión por sus rampas obligó a los fabricantes a dotar a sus máquinas de mayor potencia y mejores transmisiones. La carrera Senior tuvo como dominadora a la marca americana Indian, toda una llamada de atención para las fábricas británicas.

La Primera Guerra Mundial marcó un paréntesis de cinco años en la disputa de la competición; el TT volvió a celebrarse en 1920 en el mismo circuito de la montaña utilizado hoy en día, cuyo trazado tiene una longitud de 37,73 millas (60,72 km). Las motos evolucionaban muy rápidamente y el TT se convirtió en foco de avances tecnológicos; los ingenieros buscaban la velocidad y fiabilidad necesarias para lograr el éxito en el TT. En 1926 se consiguió por primera vez hacer una vuelta al circuito a 70 mi/h (112,7 km/h) de media; cinco años después se superó la barrera de las 80 mi/h (128,7km/h).

Las altísimas velocidades conseguidas en los años 30 convirtieron al TT en uno de los eventos más espectaculares del mundo y las hazañas de la elite de los superpilotos eran seguidas por infinidad de fans. Entre los pilotos míticos se encuentran el astuto y genial irlandés Stanley Woods, el bravo Scot Jimmy Guthrie, el rudo Freddie Frith, natural de Lincolnshire, y Jimmy Simpson, quien logró batir el récord de vuelta cinco veces aunque solo ganó una carrera. Los fabricantes británicos como Excelsior, Norton, Rudge y Velocette se alzaron en aquellos años con la mayoría de victorias, si bien las italianas Moto Guzzi y Benelli y las alemanas BMW y DKW también consiguieron triunfos en el TT.

Harold Daniell ostentaba el récord absoluto de vuelta rápida (91 mi/h) cuando la Segunda Guerra Mundial obligó a interrumpir la celebración de carreras durante 7 años. Aunque su Norton de 500 cc de fábrica

Senior TT, 1933

estaba más evolucionada que las máquinas comerciales de la época, no debe olvidarse que el trazado al que se enfrentaba Daniell era más angosto, sinuoso y bacheado que el actual y enormemente exigente con las suspensiones y los estrechos neumáticos.

La competición se reanudó en 1947, momento en el que la isla gozaba de un gran auge turístico. La gasolina de baja calidad no permitió al principio alcanzar grandes marcas por vuelta; en 1950 la joven y prometedora estrella Geoff Duke dejó el récord en 93,53 mi/h sobre una Norton que montaba un bastidor de excelente estabilidad apodado "featherbed" (el colchón de plumas).

En 1949 la FIM (Federación Internacional de Motociclismo) instauró el Campeonato del Mundo de Velocidad y la prueba más exigente del calendario era la celebrada en la isla; en ella buscaban el triunfo más de 20 fabricantes europeos. Italia mostraba su supremacía: en los años 50 Benelli, Gilera, Mondial, Moto Guzzi y MV Agusta obtuvieron un total de 26 victorias en todas las categorías individuales. El Golden Jubilee TT de 1957 fue testigo de las ansiadas primeras vueltas a 100 mi/h de media, conseguidas en la carrera Senior por el intrépido Scot Bob McIntyre sobre una Gilera, en la única edición

disputada a ocho vueltas (302 millas/486 km).

Aunque en aquel momento nadie fuera consciente de ello, la irrupción en 1959 de las pequeñas motos de 125 cc fabricadas por la entonces poco conocida Honda iba a abrir paso a una nueva era de dominio japonés. A mediados de los años 60 las colinas de la isla retumbaban con los escapes abiertos de los motores de hasta seis cilindros de las Honda, Yamaha y Suzuki en su lucha por la supremacía. Mike Hailwood consiguió la primera victoria japonesa en la prueba Senior de 1966 a lomos de una Honda.

"Mike the Bike" fue la más fulgurante de las estrellas de la galaxia de las leyendas de los grandes premios en los TT de los años 60, consiguiendo 12 victorias entre 1961 y 1967. Otros campeones mundiales que brillaron en la isla durante esa década fueron Bill Ivy, Gary Hocking, Giacomo Agostini, Hugh Anderson, Jim Redman, Luigi Taveri, Phil Read y los pilotos de sidecares Fritz Scheidegger, Helmut Fath y Max Deubel.

El duelo titánico que mantuvieron Hailwood (Honda) y Agostini (MV) en la Senior a seis vueltas de 1967 está considerado uno de los más emocionantes de la historia del TT. Ambos pilotos marcaron vueltas a velocidades récord de 108 mi/h hasta que el italiano rompió la cadena de su máquina en la quinta vuelta.

Honda abandonó el Mundial a finales de 1967 y Hailwood se retiró. Ya con menos oposición, "Ago" se hizo con otras nueve victorias para completar su palmarés de 10 triunfos. Yamaha mantuvo su equipo un año más y en 1968 Bill Ivy, piloto de la fábrica, fue el primero en marcar una vuelta a una velocidad media de 100 mi/h con una moto de 125 cc con motor de dos tiempos y cuatro cilindros. A partir de 1969 se incorporaron nuevas normas al reglamento que restringían el número de cilindros y las relaciones de marchas en cada cilindrada.

Aunque el TT se alzó como uno de los principales acontecimientos motociclistas del mundo en los años 70, las carreras afrontaban una crisis. El circuito de la montaña era uno de los últimos trazados urbanos clásicos que se mantenían en el calendario del Campeonato del Mundo y arreciaban las críticas por los enormes riesgos que asumían los pilotos. El fallecimiento del debutante Gilberto Parlotti tras una caída en una carretera mojada en 1972 llevó a Agostini y a otras primeras espadas del campeonato a boicotear el TT. La FIM retiró al TT la condición de prueba puntuable para el Campeonato del Mundo de Velocidad

tras 1976; no obstante se instauró un nuevo formato, que incluía campeonatos TT (aprobados por la FIM) para motos derivadas de serie en las categorías Formula 1, 2 y 3, lo que puso a esta cita en la senda de la recuperación. Con mucho más dinero en premios, varios pilotos británicos e irlandeses de máximo nivel decidieron especializarse en el TT.

En 1978 el sensacional regreso de Hailwood atrajo al TT a un multitudinario público, que pudo disfrutar de su inolvidable victoria sobre una Ducati en la categoría de Formula 1 frente a Phil Read y su Honda, uno de los pilotos que había boicoteado la prueba y que regresó a la isla en 1977 adjudicándose la prueba de F1.

La categoría de Formula 1, con motos de cuatro tiempos de grandes cilindradas, aumentó tanto su popularidad entre el público como su importancia para las fábricas, asegurándose así una larga existencia. Se corrió por última vez en 2004 y fue sustituida por la categoría similar denominada Superbike. Joey Dunlop, la leyenda por antonomasia del TT, ganó siete carreras de la categoría Formula 1 entre 1983 y 2000, seis de ellas consecutivas. Este tranquilo norirlandés, que corrió para Honda en la mayoría de sus numerosas apariciones en el TT, se ganó el cariño de los aficionados de las dos ruedas gracias a su increíble pericia, generosidad y enorme

Stan Woods, Ballaugh Bridge, 1957

humildad. Scot Steve Hislop fue otro de los pilotos favoritos del público, todo un maestro en la "montaña" que consiguió marcar la primera vuelta oficial a 120 mi/h en la prueba de F1 de 1989 sobre una Honda de 750 cc Desgraciadamente, ambos pilotos fallecieron en accidentes, si bien fuera de la isla.

Una epidemia de fiebre aftosa en las explotaciones ganaderas del Reino Unido trajo consigo la cancelación de las carreras en 2001, lo que supuso un punto y aparte en el brillante palmarés del popular y extraordinario David Jefferies. David obtuvo tres victorias en 1999 con Yamaha, otras tres en 2000 también con Yamaha, año en que además consiguió ser el primero en realizar una vuelta a 125 mi/h de media, y tres más en 2002, esta vez con Suzuki. La trágica muerte de David en una sesión de entrenamientos de la edición de 2003 ensombreció el TT de aquel año.

No era la primera vez en que la competición se veía abocada a un futuro incierto. Pero el gobierno de la Isla de Man y la Auto-Cycle Union (ACU), el organismo que regula las competiciones motociclistas en el Reino Unido, consiguieron salvar la situación, a lo que contribuyeron además la notable asistencia de público a dos centenarios, el del propio TT en 2007 y el del circuito de la montaña en 2011. Ningún piloto está obligado a tomar parte en las carreras; todos aquellos que disfrutan del circuito de la montaña son bienvenidos y los buscadores de talentos para el TT asisten a citas en otros lugares donde se corre en "carreteras de verdad". Actualmente no compiten moteros "vacacionales"; los pilotos del TT son profundamente respetados en el mundillo de los deportes de motor. La excelente cobertura televisiva ha contribuido a avivar el interés mundial por el TT.

La última generación de leyendas del TT incluye, entre otros, a John McGuinness, con 20 victorias entre 1999 y 2013, Michael Dunlop, integrante de la increíble dinastía Dunlop, y la figura de la televisión Guy Martin. Otras incipientes estrellas a las que no perder de vista son James Hillier y Josh Brookes. Las grandes marcas japonesas han dominado la competición en los últimos años; no obstante, la tecnología norteamericana manda en la carrera de "emisiones cero" que se celebra desde 2009 y reservada a prototipos eléctricos.

El Isle of Man Festival of Motorcycling, que empezó a celebrarse en 2013, surgió a partir del tradicional Manx Grand Prix de finales de verano, reservado a pilotos de motoclubs y a todos aquellos que deseaban introducirse en el mundo de las carreras previo al TT. El Manx GP, que comenzó a disputarse en 1930, vino a sustituir al Amateur TT (celebrado entre 1923 y 1929), e incluía carreras de motos siguiendo el formato histórico de competición de los años 80.

El punto fuerte del festival de agosto es el Classic TT, una cita internacional en la que toman parte estrellas actuales del TT y legendarios participantes de la prueba pilotando máquinas de época y réplicas; además, las carreras del Manx GP siguen siendo un buen trampolín para futuros pilotos TT y banco de pruebas para los no profesionales. Otras actividades del festival son el día de la velocidad y el ruido en Jurby, un circuito corto en la parte norte de la isla que ocupa un antiguo aeródromo, el Manx Two-Day Trial, celebrado en algunos de los puntos más remotos y pintorescos de la isla, y el Manx Classic Trial.

Las últimas carreras automovilísticas se celebraron entre 1947 y 1953 en un circuito de 3,8 millas que discurría por la actual tribuna principal ("grandstand") del TT. Desde los años 60 la isla alberga muchas de las rallies automovilísticos más exigentes de Gran Bretaña.

Aunque no es tan conocida mundialmente como el TT, la reunión motociclista Southern 100 celebrada en el circuito de Billown durante cuatro días del mes de julio es un muy agradable evento lleno de acción que nadie debe perderse. Celebrada por primera vez en 1955 –con un trazado de 100 millas para la carrera principal de 500 cc–, esta reunión cuenta con carreras nocturnas con gran ambiente motero. Entre sus ganadores individuales se cuentan Bob McIntyre, Charlie Williams y cuatro miembros de la familia Dunlop. El difunto Joey Dunlop ganó como mínimo 42 carreras de la Southern 100.

Al igual que algunas competiciones irlandesas, la Southern 100 combina las dificultades y riesgos de las vías públicas con la emoción del "rueda a rueda" de las parrillas de salida. El circuito, de 4,25 millas de longitud (6,44 km), tiene una forma semejante a un cuadrado y consta de cuatro curvas cerradas de derechas, una larga recta de bajada e infinidad de "eses", virajes y rasantes. Al igual que sucede con el trazado de la montaña, este recorrido está trufado de bordillos, muros de piedra y postes de teléfono, solo que en este circuito se rueda sobre vías más estrechas. La línea de salida, la de meta y el paddock están situados a las afueras de la histórica

Ian Lougher, Glen Vin

localidad de Castletown. En Billown tienen lugar además otros dos importantes eventos durante la celebración del TT: las Pre TT Classic Road Races y las Post TT Road Races.

Sidecares

Las carreras de motos con sidecar aportan mayor diversidad y espectáculo al TT. Alejados de la combinación tradicional de motocicleta con sidecar acoplado que se utiliza para carretera, estos vehículos de carreras son más bien proyectiles asimétricos de gran sofisticación técnica.

Los pilotos conducen con gran valentía entre setos y bordillos, mientras los "paquetes" se cuelgan literalmente del vehículo, cambiando el peso de sitio para obtener mayor estabilidad a velocidades de hasta 135 mi/h. Son pruebas que encantan a los espectadores, especialmente en los tramos más revirados o bacheados del circuito.

Disputado por primera vez entre 1923 y 1925, el Sidecar TT regresó entre 1954 y 1959 al circuito de Clypse de 10,79 millas (utilizado para algunas categorías), pasando a celebrarse de forma permanente en el circuito de la montaña a partir de 1960. En su formato actual los motores son de serie y tienen 600 centímetros cúbicos.

Categorías individuales actuales del TT

Superbike: motos adscritas al formato internacional de Superbike. Motores de dos cilindros y un máximo de 1200cc, o motores de tres o cuatro cilindros y un máximo de 1000cc

Superstock: motos de serie con limitación de cilindrada,

al igual que en Superbike.

Supersport: motos de serie en las que se permiten algunas modificaciones. Cilindrada s máximas: bicilíndricas hasta 750cc, tricilíndricas hasta 675cc y tetracilíndricas hasta 600cc

Lightweight: Motos bicilíndricas derivadas de serie con motores de un máximo de 650cc

Senior TT: para las categorías Superbike, Supersport y Superstock, además de motos de competición pura homologadas o prototipos.

Zero TT: prototipos de motos eléctricas (solo una vuelta).

Existen tres carreras Classic TT: para motos de un máximo de 350cc, máximo de 500cc y una prueba combinada con máquinas adscritas a las categorías Formula 1 Classic y Formula 2 Classic.

LOS 10 PILOTOS CON MÁS VICTORIAS EN EL TT	
26 Joey Dunlop	(1977-2000)
20 John McGuinness	(1999 –2013)
16 Dave Molyneux, Sidecar	(1989 – 2012)
14 Mike Hailwood	(1961-1979)
11 Phillip McCallen	(1992-1997)
11 Steve Hislop	(1987-1994)
10 Giacomo Agostini	(1966-1972)
10 Ian Lougher	(1997-2009)
10 Rob Fisher, Sidecar	(1994-2002)
10 Stanley Woods	(1923-1939)

Dave Molyneux & Rick Long, TT

The TT circuit

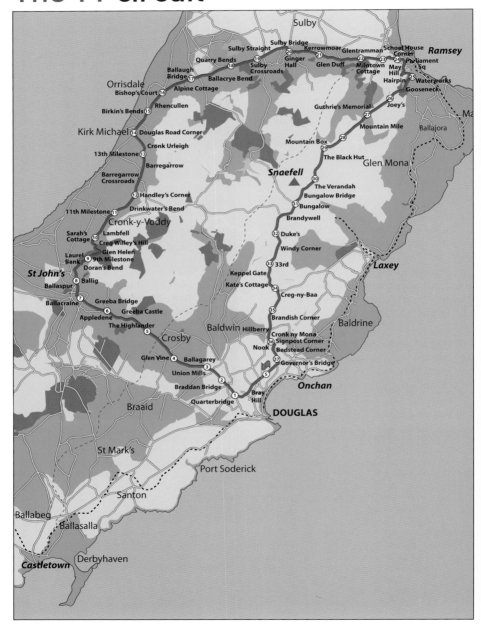

The TT and IOM Festival of Motorcycling

The 37.73-mile Mountain Course lap offers so many places to spectate that it can be difficult to decide where to go.

Regular TT visitors often have favourite spots, while newcomers are advised to try a mix of differing venues to get as full a taste of the unique atmosphere as possible during their stay. You can't cover the whole circuit in one TT, but it is possible to transfer between some vantage points while roads are closed and those fortunate enough to be on the Island during practice period can sample more locations. And there's always next time, of course!

Check road-closing times and be aware that popular free viewing places are first-come, first-served and fill up early. Wherever you are, you may be asked for a donation towards the cost of the helicopter air ambulance, or another worthy TT charity.

Do not ignore legally-binding signs marking Restricted Areas or Prohibited Areas, imposed purely in the interest of rider and spectator safety. Always be aware that when machines weighing more than 200kg are travelling at speeds approaching 200mph, the potential for an incident must be taken seriously. Respect private property and farm land, never let anything fall on the road, don't feed seagulls and please do not drop litter. Finding somewhere to park is easier with a motorcycle than a car but be careful not to cause an obstruction.

The Island's surprisingly numerous back-roads access many parts of the Course when roads are closed for racing – and provide enjoyable biking in themselves. Be aware of whether you are on the outside of the closed ring, or inside it with the obvious restriction on

🏍	**Access when roads closed**
🚫	**No access**
🅿	**Parking**
🚻	**Toilets**
🍹	**Snack and drinks**
🍴	**Lunch/dinner**
👁	**Photography tip**

movement. A link road between Quarterbridge and Braddan passes under the Course, but it is narrow and is congested with cars during races. Crossing the Course on foot is possible on bridges in Douglas, Ramsey and at the Bungalow. At some junctions, vehicles may be permitted to cross between races.

For the June TT you can buy a Fanzone ticket for entry to a grandstand on Glencrutchery Road and two other stands around the Course. Booking several months in advance is recommended.

To follow the racing and stay informed about road closures, tune in to Manx Radio TT (1368AM Island-wide, 87.9FM in Douglas and 100.6FM in the north of the island) on a radio or broadband on a smart phone or tablet. Manx Radio TT also has a Facebook page. Live race timing can be followed at www.iomtt.com from where you can download the extremely useful TT App.

CLOSE TO DOUGLAS
The Grandstand, Glencrutchery Road

The paid-for 1000-seat Grandstand may not be the best place to see spectacular bike action, but you are assured an excellent view of the start, refuelling stops, riders taking the chequered flag and the podium ceremony for the first three finishers. Audible commentary is everywhere, while binoculars are useful for following riders' progress on the ancient scoreboard operated by Boy Scouts and Cubs. Roam the TT Village behind the grandstand and enjoy a festive atmosphere with catering outlets, a bar tent and merchandise area.

It is recommended that main Grandstand tickets be pre-booked, but if they're not sold out, some will be on sale at a kiosk on racedays. A 300-seat ticket holders' stand in Nobles Park overlooks the lane where finishing riders return to the paddock, as well as the Course. ✦ P ✗ wc 👁 a chance to get close to riders and machines.

For a full hospitality package with privileged access to riders and information on racedays, VIP area tickets can be pre-booked for a little over £300.

Hillberry and Cronk-ny-Mona
See riders approach at high speed from Brandish Corner ¾ mile (one kilometre) away and tear round the right-hand Hillberry bend at 150mph, trying not to go too wide on the exit. There is a paid-for grandstand on the outside of the Course with basic toilet facilities. A back road connects Hilberry with School Road, Onchan which is off the main A2 route.

Cronk-ny-Mona is a speedy leftward sweep, with viewing only possible on the outside of the Course where a junction with both the A21 and a minor road provide links to numerous other vantage points along the first few miles (kilometres of the lap) via the network of roads inside the Course. ✦ P on narrow backroad, be prepared for a walk. 👁 pan from outside corner.

Signpost Corner and Bedstead Corner
A roundabout when roads are open, Signpost is a relatively slow (80mph/129km/h) right-hand turn coming straight after a blind crest and followed by the bedstead left turn. A private house overlooking Signpost is open to the public, who should make a donation to the Helicopter Fund. ✦ By A39 from junction with A18 by Manx Arms pub in Onchan. ⚡ P wc 👁 pan from outside corner.

Cameron Donald, Hillberry, TT

Governor's Bridge
A tricky dead-slow right-hand hairpin followed by a leftward curve through shaded Governor's Dip and an uphill exit to the right onto Glencrutchery Road. There's standing room to see the hairpin from the main A18 road to Onchan and B34 back road. No spectating in the Dip, but the Victoria Road junction gives a good view of riders accelerating out of the last corner before the finish line.
 P

St Ninian's crossroads
Wheels rise off the tarmac as bikes bank left through the crossroads and aim for the Bray Hill descent at 170mph. Can be tight for standing room with good views, but easy to get to from downtown Douglas and offers the convenience of a footbridge and service station with a shop.
 ✗ P

Bray Hill
Breathtaking! Machines plummet down the slope at 180mph or more, to veer left through the five-way junction at the bottom, as the suspension is fully squashed. A free area with a great view at the foot of the hill beside Stoney Road fills up quickly. There is a stand on the opposite side of the road and free viewing from the ends of Thorney Road, Cronkbourne Road on the outside of the course and Tromode Road on the inside.

Higher up, you can watch from side roads on the outside of the Course, but won't get a long view. Further on, there is limited space on private property to watch riders wheelie along Quarterbridge Road as they emerge from out of the dip at the foot of the hill. Get permission and turn up very early.

➔ ⚡ wc P but not very close to the Course. 👁 difficult to get good shots from public areas without professional equipment.

Quarterbridge
Riders must brake hard for this tight right-hander, the first true corner after the start and a roundabout on open roads. You get close to the action alongside the hospitable Quarterbridge Pub, but have to look through high mesh safety fencing. There is also spectator space across the road, by the white flat-roofed building. Closed roads access and parking are no problem.
➔ ✗ wc P

Braddan Bridge
A sharp right over the bridge is followed by a sweeping left and a rightward kink. For spectating on the outside of the course choose from two separately owned paid-for enclosures. Tiered seating for around 400 overlooks the main bends, while a smaller number of seats in Braddan church grounds overlook the left kink where riders accelerate hard away. Both sites offer catering and toilets, although the church scores highly with homemade food in the church hall and permanent conveniences with disabled access and baby-changing.

There is free viewing area with limited space in the grounds of the Old Church.
➔ ✗ P

UNION MILLS TO ST JOHN'S
Union Mills
The friendly Railway Inn, standing on the outside of the Course beside the B32 Lhergy Cripperty side-road, overlooks the right-hand curve in the road as it falls downhill towards the left-hander in the village. A recently enlarged the beer garden provides a good vantage point.

Alternatively, see riders sweep through the tricky 120mph left-hander from the grounds of the Church Hall, where refreshments are served, or the Memorial Hall near the Strang Road junction on the inside of the Course. There is a convenience store by the junction that closes when racing is on.
➔ ✗ P early arrival advised. 👁 Exceptional shots can be taken here, especially with a long lens.

Ballahutchin straight
Keen spectators find spots on the outside of the course, note restricted areas. ⊘

Crosby
A flat-out 180mph-plus stretch through the village, with viewing from junctions with the B35 (outside Course) or A23 (inside). For comfort and convenience, the Crosby Hotel pub, which has a parking area, is the best option, but note that there's no entry or exit while the roads are closed. ⊘ ✕ P wc

The Highlander
Bikes can be nudging 200mph on this straight downhill section passing the Highlander restaurant, which has a parking area on the opposite side of the road.

Snacks, as well as meals, available but no entry or exit when roads are closed. ⊘ ✕ P wc

The Hawthorn
The pub specialising in food has spectating room along its frontage, from where you can see riders changing up as they accelerate out of the Greeba Bridge left-hander. ⊘ ✕ P wc

Knock Breck Farm, Greeba
The hospitable owner of this property, passed by racers at 160mph-plus, not only allows access to his front garden and farmyard, but offers homemade refreshments. Please respect hospitality.
➥ by a lane off the A3 road half a mile south from Ballacraine, passing Kennaa equestrian centre. ✕ P wc

Ballacraine
A sharp right-turn close to St John's, where spectators can watch from outside the Course at the junction with the A3 road, or for a better view, on a bank beside the road.
👁 Good opportunities for photos.

Nearby St John's has a shop, pub and a licensed cafe/restaurant in the village and a small shopping area at nearby Tynwald Mills has two cafes. ➥ ✕ P

GLEN HELEN TO BALLAUGH
Glen Helen corner
The Glen Helen pub's spacious parking area looks onto a 110mph left-hander where the twisty road that has threaded through the glen starts a steep climb.

Cameron Donald & Conor Cummins, Hawthorn, TT

As well as the pub, which usually offers a barbecue during races, there is the Swiss Chalet restaurant. A high bank on the outside of the corner, where one of the Manx Radio commentary boxes is sited, offers free spectating.

The adventurous can walk off-road on the inside of the course back towards Black Dub where some parking is also available. Be aware of prohibited areas.

🚫 🚽 ✂ P 👁 shoot from the high bank near the commentary box at Glen Helen for an unusual angle.

Cronk-y-Voddy

An undulating straight where high speed is reached before a right kink just after the crossroads: watch how the best riders shut off less than the others. 🚗 by narrow lanes on both sides of the course. ✂ P for a small fee. 🚽

Barregarrow

Scary stuff. Limited room for spectators at the top of the hill, where back roads offer access. 🚗 at top, from inside course. 🚽

Kirk Michael

The Course enters the village at Douglas Road Corner, where you can watch at the A4 junction on the outside. Further along, the Mitre pub on the inside overlooks the exit, where riders accelerate down the narrow main street. 🚫 ✂ 🚽

Further down the village you can see machines hurtle towards you at around 180mph from a small paid-for spectating area at Whitehouse Park. 🚫 ✂ P 🚽 👁 opportunities from a bank on the outside of Douglas Road corner. For breathtaking village street action, park at Glen Wyllin campsite and take the footpath along the old railway line, to access Station Road or, via a stairway, Bayr ny Balleira. Both adjoin the Course where you can stand behind barriers. Long lenses are needed for the best results.

Rhencullen

Limited spectating on this terrifying section with twists and wheel-lofting crests. Access by lanes via Orrisdale from outside of the Course.

Obey marshals' instructions. 🚗 🚽 P for a small fee.

Ballaugh Bridge

Everyone should go here at least once, to watch riders leap off the famous hump-backed bridge. You can see most from behind the barriers on the outside of the Course and can access to a convenience store.

🚗 outside the Course by back roads to vantage points at Sulby, as well as routes leading to Ramsey and Douglas.

🚗 inside Course to Brandywell, Barregarrow by scenic mountain roads, access Douglas area/Union Mills via Injebreck.
✂ P 🚽

The convivial Raven Inn across the road obviously has its attractions. 🚫 ✂ P 🚽 👁 arrive early for a spot behind barriers opposite the pub. If it is crowded you may need a box or steps to stand on for an unobstructed view.

Ballacrye

Super-fast left curve and a crest that lifts front wheels high. A tickets-only Fanzone stand here accommodates 200 ticket holders. 🚫 🚽 🚽

SULBY TO RAMSEY
Sulby Glen

The welcoming Sulby Glen pub stands outside the Course on a crossroads at the bumpy start of the super-fast Sulby Straight, where the fastest riders wind up to around 190mph. Viewing is also possible from barriers on the A14 road that cross the straight and a shop selling light refreshments is on the inside of the Course, where the A14 connects with Ginger

> On non racing days, a wide range of events is held throughout the island at Ramsey, Laxey, Peel and Port Erin.
> On the Tuesday of race week (weather permitting) the famous Ramsey sprint – a drag event over an 1/8 mile takes place.
> Readers are advised to listen to Manx Radio or Radio TT for further information on these events and others, or see the official TT entertainment website www.iomtt.com

Hall and the Bungalow. On the outside of the Course it links with Sulby Bridge and the Island's northern road network.

⮌ Vehicles can cross under direction during intervals in racing.
✕ P wc

Sulby Bridge

Hard braking is needed to cut terrific speed gained on the straight in order to get round the tight right-hander. There is a paid-for stand (not a Fanzone) and some room for spectating on the outside of the course before the corner and from the barrier at the A17 road junction.

👁 tremendous opportunities for photos with impact. Shoot from the hedge before the bridge, looking towards Sulby village.
⮌ zZ P wc

Dan Cooper & Davy Morgan, Ginger Hall, TT

Ginger Hall

A left-hand bend taken at about 120mph with the congenial Ginger Hall pub on the outside, where a back road connecting with Sulby Glen and The Bungalow joins the Course. Viewing from outside the pub, or even through the window, and parking is available in the pub car park or the side road.

🏍 ✕ P wc 👁 Bikes are close to the right-hand kerb before swinging across to the apex, helping photographers get good shots from several spots near the pub.

Churchtown, Lezayre

A fast and very spectacular stretch, with good viewing from area known as 'conker trees' on the inside of the course. It overlooks a projecting kerb that a letter K painted on a tree warns riders about. A loop road running past Lezayre Church can be used for parking. No access when roads are closed.

🚫 🍴 P near church. wc

👁 Photographers with media passes have no advantage here! You'll need a short/medium telephoto lens and a fast shutter speed. With anything other than a professional standard DSLR you need to focus manually using a spot on the road that the bike go over, then press the button an instant before they pass over it.

If you are in the north of the Island, don't miss the TT Teas that have been served up since 1993. They are laid on at the church hall in the village of Bride by ladies of the parish

RAMSEY AREA
Parliament Square

Situated in Ramsey town, these slow bends attract crowds. There are two pubs, the Central and the Swan, right on the course, plus numerous stores, fish & chip shops and other food outlets in the vicinity. Riders must brake hard to negotiate a sharp right turn into the square and a gentle left on the exit. Spectators can stand in front of the Town Hall, or use limited room at the end of a back lane leading off the Square. Side roads on either side give a view of the exit onto a short straight.

🏍 P ✕ wc 👁 Low speeds help photographers. If you don't zoom in close, backgrounds provide unique TT atmosphere.

Cruikshanks

A treacherous uphill right-hander leading on to bumpy May Hill, taken at up to 120mph. Good views of the bend from both sides of the road with a footbridge nearby. You can also watch on the hill, from side openings on either side of the Course accessed by back lanes. Close to A18 Ramsey to Douglas road and Manx Electric Railway terminus. 🏍 P

Ramsey Hairpin

Very slow hairpin under trees overlooked by Manx Radio's second commentary point. Limited space for spectators and parking nearby can be a problem. Access from A18 by a lane on the left beside the Ballure MER tram crossing. 🏍

The Mountain Section

Glorious in fine weather, the A16 road that climbs out of Ramsey and traverses the uninhabited highlands before descending towards Douglas offers many vantage points, both easily accessible and isolated.

The Gooseneck

A sharp right-hander, as the name suggests, on the climb from Ramsey, with fabulous sea views in fine weather. Great braking and cornering action and riders can be seen approaching for some distance. Closed road access by narrow D28 track from easy-to miss junction on A2 at the Hibernian. Pay to park in a field, some free parking for bikes in lane. 🏍 🍴 P wc 👁 great opportunities for photos or video.

The Bungalow

Sweeping bends with a tramline crossing and long views in both directions and footbridge. Take the scenic A14 road from here to reach Sulby Glen or Ginger Hall inside the course. Or arrive on the Snaefell Mountain Railway from Laxey, which you can also take to the cafe at the summit. 🏍 🍴 P wc

It is possible to walk along the side of the Course from here, but beware of soft peat bogs.

🏴󠁧󠁢󠁥󠁮󠁧󠁿

👁 lots of different angles possible, including really scenic shots from outside the Course beyond the bends towards Brandywell.

Brandywell

This left-hander taken at 100mph-plus sorts Mountain masters from the rest, just beyond Hailwood Heights, the highest point on the Course. Exposed in poor weather, refreshments not guaranteed, no toilets. Parking along B10 road, which connects with Barregarrow and Douglas (via Injebreck) on scenic roads and with Ballaugh Bridge via a single-track asphalted moorland road.

🚗 🍴 P

Keppel Gate/Kate's Cottage

Where the Mountain descent really starts, with a left-hander followed by the drop down to a blind leftward kink by the isolated cottage taken at over 100mph. Spring water often dampens the road on the racing line.

Good long views from the upper section, and the bank opposite the cottage can be reached by walking ½mile (750m) up a narrow path from Creg-ny-Baa.

A much longer trek alongside the course takes you on to the leftward sweeps at the 33rd Milestone, the Windy Corner left-hander and three fast left kinks at Duke's. 🚗 P 👁 lots of interesting angles, take care to stay in permitted areas.

Creg-ny-Baa

A pub/restaurant attracts crowds to this 80mph left-hander with a fabulous view up the bumpy straight dropping down from Kate's. There are two grandstands, a private venture (small fee) overlooking the entry to the bend and a 400-seat Fanzone on the exit. Closed-roads access via the B12 which has a junction with the A2 about ¾mile (one kilometre) beyond Onchan.

🚗 ✕ P WC 👁 The best positions are on the outside, on the approach to bend looking back towards Kate's.

Jason Griffiths, Bungalow, TT

Die TT und das IOM
Festival of Motorcycling

Die 60,7 km lange Bergstrecke bietet so viele Orte zum Zuschauen, dass es schwierig sein kann, eine Entscheidung zu treffen.

Wer die TT regelmäßig besucht, hat oft einen Lieblingsort. Neuankömmlingen wird dagegen empfohlen, unterschiedliche Orte auszuprobieren, damit sie die einzigartige Atmosphäre während ihres Aufenthalts möglichst umfassend erleben können. Man kann während einer TT zwar nicht die ganze Strecke besuchen, aber es ist möglich, die Aussichtspunkte zu wechseln, während die Straßen gesperrt sind. Wer das Glück hat, bereits während des Trainings auf der Insel zu sein, kann mehrere Orte ausprobieren. Außerdem gibt es immer ein nächstes Mal!

Achten Sie darauf wann die Straßen gesperrt werden und denken Sie daran, dass beliebte kostenlose Aussichtspunkte schnell voll sind, denn es gilt: wer zuerst kommt malt zuerst. Je nach dem wo Sie sich das Rennen ansehen, können Sie um eine Spende für die Ambulanzhelikopter oder einen anderen gemeinnützigen Zweck im Rahmen der TT gebeten werden.

Halten Sie sich an rechtsverbindliche Schilder, die Gebiete mit beschränktem Zutritt oder Zutrittsverbot kennzeichnen. Sie dienen ausschließlich der Sicherheit der Fahrer und Zuschauer. Schließlich ist dass Unfallpotential von über 200 kg schweren Motorrädern, die mit beinahe 320 km/h unterwegs sind, sehr ernst zu nehmen. Halten Sie die Gesetze hinsichtlich Privatgrundstücken und landwirtschaftlichen Nutzflächen ein, lassen Sie keinesfalls Gegenstände auf die Straße fallen, füttern Sie keine Möwen und lassen Sie bitte keinen Müll liegen. Mit einem Motorrad findet man leichter einen Parkplatz als mit dem Auto, aber verursachen Sie bitte keine Behinderungen.

Über die vielen Nebenstraßen auf der Insel sind viele Abschnitte der Rennstrecke erreichbar, wenn die Straßen wegen der Rennen geschlossen sind – außerdem

🚶	**Zugang bei gesperrten Straßen**
⊘	**Kein Zugang**
P	**Parkplatz**
WC	**Toiletten**
🍹	**Snacks und Getränke**
✗	**Mittagessen**
📷	**Fototipp**

sind sie schöne Fahrtrouten. Achten Sie darauf, ob sie sich außerhalb der ringförmigen Strecke befinden oder innerhalb, wo Ihre Bewegungsfreiheit natürlich eingeschränkt ist. Es gibt eine Verbindungsstraße, die zwischen Quarterbridge und Braddan unter der Strecke hindurchführt. Sie ist jedoch schmal und während der Rennen stauen sich hier die Autos. Zu Fuß kann die Rennstrecke über Brücken in Douglas, Ramsey und beim Bungalow überquert werden. Einige Kreuzungen dürfen Fahrzeuge zwischen den Rennen ggf. überqueren.

Für die TT im Juni können Sie ein Fanzone-Ticket kaufen, mit dem Sie Zugang zur Haupttribüne in der Glencrutchery Road sowie zu zwei anderen Tribünen an der Strecke haben. Wir empfehlen Ihnen, bereits einige Monate im Voraus zu buchen.

Aktuelle Informationen zum Rennen und den Straßensperren erhalten Sie von Manx Radio TT (1368 AM auf der gesamten Insel, 87,9 FM in Douglas und 100,6 FM im Norden der Insel), das Sie mit dem Radio oder per Breitband mit einem Smartphone oder Tablet empfangen können. Manx Radio TT hat auch eine Facebook-Seite. Auf www.iomtt.com können Sie das Live Timing der Rennen verfolgen. Dort können Sie sich auch die praktische TT-App herunterladen.

IN DER UMGEBUNG VON DOUGLAS
Die Haupttribüne, Glencrutchery Road

Die kostenpflichtige Haupttribüne mit 1000 Plätzen ist zwar nicht der besten Ort, um spektakuläre Motorrad-Action zu sehen, aber Sie haben einen hervorragenden Blick auf den Start, auf Tankstopps, wie die Fahrer das Signal mit der Zielflagge erhalten und auf die Siegerehrung der drei Bestplatzierten. Der Kommentar ist überall hörbar und mit Ferngläsern lässt sich der Fortschritt der Fahrer gut auf der alten Anzeigetafel verfolgen, die von Pfadfindern bedient wird. Besuchen Sie das TT-Dorf hinter der Tribüne und genießen

Sie die Festatmosphäre mit Imbissständen, einem Barzelt und einem Bereich mit Fanartikeln.

Wir empfehlen, Tickets für die Haupttribüne im Voraus zu kaufen, aber wenn sie noch nicht ausverkauft sind, sind sie an den Renntagen an der Kasse erhältlich. Eine Tribüne mit 300 Sitzen für Ticketinhaber befindet sich im Nobles Park. Hier ist die Straße über die die Fahrer ins Fahrerlager zurückkehren, und die Rennstrecke sichtbar. ⟵ P ✕ wc ◉ Eine Gelegenheit dicht an die Fahrer und Maschinen heranzukommen.

Ein Komplettpaket mit Vorzugszugang zu den Fahrern, Informationen an Renntagen und Karten für den VIP-Bereich kann für etwas über 300 £ vorbestellt werden.

Hillberry und Cronk-ny-Mona
Hier sehen Sie die Fahrer mit Höchstgeschwindigkeit von der einen Kilometer entfernten Brandish Corner herannahen und mit ca. 240 Sachen um die Hillberry-Rechtskurve rasen, wobei sie sich nicht zu weit nach außen tragen lassen dürfen. Es gibt eine kostenpflichtige große Tribüne an der Außenseite der Strecke mit einfachen Toiletten. Eine Nebenstraße verbindet Hillberry mit der School Road in Onchan, die von der A2 abzweigt.

Cronk-ny-Mona ist eine schnelle Linksbiegung, die nur von der Außenseite der Strecke eingesehen werden kann, wo eine Kreuzung der A21 und einer kleinen Straße über ein Straßennetz innerhalb der Strecke Zugang zu vielen anderen Aussichtspunkten entlang der ersten Kilometer der Strecke bietet.
⟵ P Auf schmaler Nebenstraße, ggf. mit Fußmarsch.
◉ Panoramablick von Kurvenaußenseite.

Signpost Corner und Bedstead Corner
Wenn die Straßen offen sind, handelt es sich bei der Signpost Corner um einen Verkehrskreisel. Während der Rennen ist sie eine relativ langsame (ca. 130 km/h) Rechtskurve direkt hinter einer nicht einsehbaren Kuppe, auf die direkt die Bedstead-Linkskurve folgt. Ein Privatgebäude mit Blick auf Signpost Corner ist der Öffentlichkeit zugänglich, hier wird um eine Spende für die Ambulanzhelikopter gebeten. ⟵ An der A39 hinter der Kreuzung mit der A18 am Manx Arms Pub in Onchan. ⚡ P wc ◉ Panoramablick von Kurvenaußenseite.

Governor's Bridge
Eine schwierige, sehr langsame Haarnadelkurve, auf die die schattige Governor's-Dip-Linkskurve und eine ansteigende Ausfahrt nach rechts auf die Glencrutchery

Michael Dunlop, St Ninian's Cross Roads, TT

Road folgen. An der A18 nach Onchan und der Nebenstraße B34 gibt es Stehplätze mit Sicht auf die Haarnadelkurve. Zu Governor's Dip haben Zuschauer keinen Zugang, aber die Kreuzung der Victoria Road bietet einen guten Blick auf die Fahrer, die die letzte Kurve verlassen und vor der Ziellinie beschleunigen. ↩ P

St-Ninian's-Kreuzung
Wenn die Motorräder auf der Kreuzung nach links biegen und mit 270 km/h auf den Abstieg von Bray Hill zufahren, lösen sich die Räder von der Fahrbahn. Relativ wenige Stehplätze mit guter Sicht, aber leicht vom Zentrum von Douglas aus zu erreichen. Außerdem gibt es eine Fußgängerbrücke und Tankstelle mit Geschäft. ↩ ✗ P

Bray Hill
Atemberaubend! Die Maschinen rasen den Hang mit 290 km/h und mehr hinunter, schwenken dann nach rechts ein und überqueren die Fünffach-Kreuzung mit komplett zusammengedrückter Aufhängung. Es gibt einen kostenlosen Bereich mit toller Sicht am Fuß des Hügels neben der Stoney Road, der jedoch schnell voll ist. Auf der gegenüberliegenden Straßenseite gibt es eine Tribüne und an der Streckenaußenseite kann man am Ende der Thorney Road und Cronkbourne Road sowie an der Streckeninnenseite in der Tromode Road kostenlos zuschauen.

Von höher gelegenen Nebenstraßen außerhalb der Strecke hat man ebenfalls Sicht, kann die Strecke aber nicht so weit einsehen. Etwas weiter die Strecke hinunter steht begrenzter Platz auf einem Privatgrundstück zur Verfügung, dort sieht man die Fahrer auf dem Hinterrad die Quarterbridge Road passieren, wenn sie die Senke am Fuß des Hügels verlassen. Bitten Sie hier um Erlaubnis zum Betreten des Grundstücks und seien Sie sehr zeitig da. ↩ ⚑ wc P Jedoch nicht nah an der Strecke.
👁 Ohne Profiausrüstung kann man nur schwer gute Bilder von öffentlichen Bereichen aus machen.

Quarterbridge
Vor dieser engen Rechtsbiegung müssen die Fahrer stark bremsen. Es ist die erste richtige Kurve nach dem Start und einem Verkehrskreisel auf offener Strecke. Neben dem gemütlichen Quarterbridge Pub sind Sie ganz nah

am Geschehen, müssen allerdings durch eine engmaschige Sicherheitsumzäunung schauen. Auch auf der gegenüberliegenden Straßenseite gibt es an dem weißen Gebäude mit Flachdach Platz für Zuschauer. Zugang bei gesperrten Straßen und Parkplätze sind vorhanden. ↩ ✗ wc P

Braddan Bridge
Auf eine steile Rechtskurve auf der Brücke folgen eine lange Linksbiegung und ein Rechtsknick. An der Außenseite der Strecke kann man von zwei kostenpflichtigen eingezäunten Bereichen aus zusehen. Es gibt abgestufte Sitzplätze für etwa 400 Personen über den Hauptkurven und einige Sitzplätze auf dem Braddan-Kirchengelände bieten einen Blick auf den Linksknick, auf dem die Fahrer kräftig beschleunigen. An beiden Orten gibt es Verpflegung und Toiletten, wobei die Kirche mit hausgemachtem Essen im Gemeindesaal und festen Toiletteneinrichtungen mit Behindertenzugang und Wickelraum punktet.

Auf dem Gelände der Old Church gibt es einen kleinen kostenlosen Zuschauerbereich. ↩ ✗ P

VON UNION MILLS NACH ST JOHN'S
Union Mills
Der freundliche Railway Inn auf der Außenseite der Strecke an der Nebenstraße Lhergy Cripperty (B32) blickt auf die Rechtskurve nach der die abfallende Straße auf die Linkskurve im Dorf zuführt. Der kürzlich vergrößerte Biergarten ist ein guter Aussichtspunkt.

Alternativ können Sie auch zuschauen, wie die Fahrer mit ca. 190 km/h die schwierige Linkskurve durchqueren. Auf dem Gelände der Church Hall werden Erfrischungen angeboten, man kann auch auf der

An den Tagen, an denen keine Rennen stattfinden, gibt es zahlreiche Veranstaltungen in Ramsey, Laxey, Peel und Port Erin. Am Dienstag der Rennwoche findet bei gutem Wetter der berühmte Ramsey Sprint statt. Dabei handelt es sich um ein Beschleunigungsrennen über eine Strecke von ca. 200 Metern. Weitere Informationen zu dieser und anderen Veranstaltungen erhalten Sie über das Manx Radio oder Radio TT. Oder besuchen Sie die offizielle TT-Website: www.iomtt.com

Innenseite der Strecke von der Memorial Hall nahe des Abzweigs der Strang Road aus zusehen. Am Abzweig steht ein Lebensmittelladen, der während der Rennen schließt.

🏍 ✕ P Es ist ratsam, zeitig einzutreffen. 👁 Hier können außergewöhnliche Aufnahmen gemacht werden, insbesondere mit langer Brennweite.

Ballahutchin-Gerade

Außerhalb der Strecke gibt es Plätze zum Zuschauen, bitte auf gesperrte Bereiche achten. ⃠

Crosby

Auf diesem Stück durch das Dorf legen die Fahrer Geschwindigkeiten von 290 km/h und mehr vor. Das Zuschauen ist an Kreuzungen der B35 (außerhalb der Strecke) oder A23 (innerhalb der Strecke) möglich. Der Crosby Hotel Pub mit Parkplatz ist am bequemsten, aber beachten Sie, dass es keine Zufahrt oder Ausfahrt gibt, wenn die Straßen gesperrt sind. ⃠ ✕ P ꟽ

The Highlander

Auf diesem abfallenden geraden Abschnitt vorbei am Restaurant The Highlander mit Parkplatz auf der gegenüberliegenden Straßenseite können die Motorräder eine Geschwindigkeit von um die 320 km/h erreichen.

Es werden Snacks und Mahlzeiten angeboten, aber wenn die Straßen gesperrt sind, gibt es keine Zu- oder Ausfahrt. ⃠ ✕ P ꟽ

The Hawthorn

Von der Straßenfront dieses auf Essen spezialisierten Pubs sehen Sie die Fahrer einige Gänge höher schalten, wenn sie aus der Linkskurve der Greeba Bridge hinaus beschleunigen. ⃠ ✕ P ꟽ

Knock Breck Farm, Greeba

Der gastfreundliche Besitzer dieses Grundstücks, das die Rennfahrer mit 250 km/h und schneller passieren, gestattet nicht nur den Zutritt zu seinem Vorgarten und Hof, sondern bietet sogar hausgemachte Erfrischungen an. Bitte halten Sie sich an die Regeln der Gastfreundschaft.

🏍 An einer Straße, die ca. 0,8 km südlich von Ballacraine von der A3 abzweigt und am Kennaa-Pferdesportzentrum vorüberführt. ✕ P ꟽ

Ballacraine

Enge Rechtskurve bei St John's, wo Zuschauen von der Streckenaußenseite an der Kreuzung mit der A3 möglich ist. Eine bessere Sicht hat man auf einer Böschung neben der Straße.

👁 Gute Fotogelegenheit.

Im nahen St John's gibt es ein Geschäft, einen Pub und ein Café/Restaurant mit Schanklizenz und ein kleiner Einkaufspark bei Tynwald Mills hat zwei Cafés. 🏍 ✕ P

VON GLEN HELEN NACH BALLAUGH
Kurve Glen Helen

Der weitläufige Parkplatz des Glen Helen Pub blickt auf eine Linkskurve, die mit ca. 170 km/h durchfahren wird. Hier beginnt die kurvenreiche Talstraße stark anzusteigen.

Neben dem Pub, der während der Rennen für gewöhnlich ein Barbecue veranstaltet, gibt es auch das Restaurant Swiss Chalet. Auf einer hohen Böschung auf der Außenseite der Kurve befindet sich eine der Kommentatorenkabinen des Manx Radio. Hier kann man auch kostenlos zusehen.

Abenteuerlustige können innerhalb der Strecke jenseits der Wege zurück nach Black Dub gehen, wo es einige Parkplätze gibt. Achten Sie auf die gesperrten Gebiete.

⃠ ꟽ ✕ P 👁 Bei der Kommentatorenkabine von Glen Helen auf der hohen Böschung erhalten Sie Bilder mit ungewöhnlichem Blickwinkel.

Cronk-y-Voddy

Auf der hügeligen Gerade werden Höchstgeschwindigkeiten erreicht, ehe sie kurz hinter der Kreuzung in einen Rechtsknick führt. Man kann gut beobachten, dass die besten Fahrer weniger vom Gas gehen als andere. 🏍 Über schmale Straßen auf beiden Seiten der Strecke. ✕ P Gegen eine kleine Gebühr. ꟽ

Barregarrow

Beängstigend. Beschränkter Platz für Zuschauer auf dem Gipfel des Hügels mit Zugang über Seitenstraßen.

🏍 Oben, innerhalb der Strecke. ⚡

Kirk Michael

An der Douglas Road Corner führt die Strecke in das Dorf hinein. Dort können Sie an der Außenseite der

Strecke an der Kreuzung der A4 zuschauen. Ein Stück weiter bietet der Mitre Pub an der Streckeninnenseite Sicht auf das Ende der Kurve, wo die Fahrer auf der engen Hauptstraße beschleunigen. ◐ ✕ ⓌⒸ

Im Dorf können Sie von einem kleinen kostenpflichtigen Zuschauerbereich am Whitehouse Park die Maschinen mit etwa 290 km/h auf sich zurasen sehen. ◐ ✕ Ⓟ ⓌⒸ ◉ Gelegenheit zum Fotografieren auf einer Böschung außerhalb der Kurve der Douglas Road. Wenn Sie atemberaubende Action in den Straßen des Dorfes erleben möchten, parken Sie am Campingplatz Glen Wyllin und folgen Sie dem Pfad entlang der alten Bahnstrecke zur Station Road oder über eine Treppe zur Bayr ny Balleira. Beide Straßen grenzen an die Strecke und man kann hinter Absperrungen zusehen. Für gute Fotos benötigen Sie eine lange Brennweite.

Rhencullen
An diesem gefährlichen Abschnitt mit Kurven und Hügeln, durch die die Räder den Bodenkontakt verlieren, ist das Zuschauen begrenzt möglich. Außerhalb der Strecke gewähren Straßen über Orrisdale Zugang. Befolgen Sie die Anweisungen der Ordner. ↩ ☰ Ⓟ Gegen eine kleine Gebühr.

Ballaugh Bridge
Jeder sollte mindestens einmal von hier aus zuschauen, um die Fahrer von der bekannten gewölbten Brücke springen zu sehen. Die beste Sicht hat man hinter den Absperrungen außerhalb der Strecke. Außerdem gibt es einen Lebensmittelladen.
↩ von außerhalb der Strecke über Nebenstraßen zu Aussichtspunkten in Sulby sowie die Straßen nach Ramsey und Douglas.
↩ von innerhalb der Strecke nach Brandywell, Barregarrow über malerische Bergstraßen, über Injebreck Zugang ins Gebiet von Douglas/Union Mills. ✕ Ⓟ ⓌⒸ

Der gesellige Raven Inn auf der gegenüberliegenden Straßenseite ist sehr einladend. ◐ ✕ Ⓟ ⓌⒸ ◉ Um einen Platz hinter den Absperrungen gegenüber dem Pub zu ergattern, müssen Sie zeitig eintreffen. Falls es voll ist, brauchen Sie ggf. eine Kiste oder Stufe, um ungehindert sehen zu können.

Ballacrye
Superschnelle Linkskurve und ein Hügel, bei dem sich die Vorderräder von der Straße heben. Hier gibt es eine Fanzone mit 200 Plätzen, für die Tickets benötigt werden. ◐ ☰ ⓌⒸ

VON SULBY NACH RAMSEY
Sulby Glen
Der einladende Sulby Glen Pub befindet sich außerhalb der Strecke an einer Kreuzung am holprigen Anfang der rasend schnellen Sulby-Gerade. Hier drehen die schnellsten Fahrer auf bis zu 305 km/h auf. Man kann von Absperrungen an der A14 aus zusehen, die die Gerade schneidet. Innerhalb der Strecke, wo die A14 auf Ginger Hall und den Bungalow trifft, werden in einem Laden Erfrischungen verkauft. Außerhalb der Strecke ist sie mit Sulby Bridge und dem nördlichen Straßennetz der Insel verbunden. ↩ Fahrzeuge können hier während Rennpausen nach Anweisung überqueren. ✕ Ⓟ ⓌⒸ

Sulby Bridge
Hier muss stark gebremst werden, um die hohen Geschwindigkeiten, die die Fahrer auf der Geraden erreichen, beim Einfahren in die steile Rechtskurve zu senken. Es gibt eine kostenpflichtige Tribüne (keine Fanzone) und einen Zuschauerbereich außerhalb der Strecke vor der Kurve und der Absperrung an der Straßenkreuzung der A17.
◉ Man kann hier eindrückliche Bilder machen. Fotografieren Sie von der Hecke vor der Brücke aus mit Blick auf das Dorf Sulby. ↩ ☰ Ⓟ ⓌⒸ

Ginger Hall
Die Linksbiegung wird mit etwa 190 km/h durchfahren. Außerhalb der Strecke befindet sich der gemütliche Ginger Hall Pub, wo eine Nebenstraße zu Sulby Glen und dem Bungalow auf die Strecke stößt. Sie können vor dem Pub oder von innen durch ein Fenster zuschauen. Parkplätze gibt es am Pub oder in der Nebenstraße.
↩ ✕ Ⓟ ⓌⒸ ◉ Die Motorräder fahren dicht am rechten Straßenrand entlang und schwenken dann durch den Scheitelpunkt, dadurch erhalten Sie an vielen Orten am Pub gute Fotos.

Gooseneck, TT

Churchtown, Lezayre

Dieser Abschnitt ist schnell und sehr spektakulär. An einer Stelle namens „Conker Trees" innerhalb der Strecke hat man eine gute Sicht. Von dort sieht man einen vorstehenden Bordstein, vor dem die Fahrer durch ein auf einen Baum gemaltes K gewarnt werden. In einem Rundweg um die Lezayre-Kirche kann man Parken. Kein Zugang bei gesperrten Straßen.

◎ ☰ P Bei der Kirche. WC

👁 Fotografen mit Presseausweis werden hier nicht bevorzugt! Sie benötigen ein kurzes/mittleres Teleobjektiv und kurze Verschlusszeiten. Falls Sie nicht über eine Spiegelreflexkamera für Profis verfügen, fokussieren Sie manuell auf einen Punkt auf der Straße, den die Motorräder durchqueren werden. Drücken Sie den Auslöser einen Augenblick, bevor das Motorrad diesen Punkt erreicht.

Wenn Sie sich im Norden der Insel aufhalten, verpassen Sie nicht die TT Teas, die seit 1993 veranstaltet werden. Im Gemeindesaal im Dorf Bride servieren Damen aus der Gemeinde Tee und Gebäck.

GEBIET VON RAMSEY
Parliament Square

Die langsamen Kurven in der Stadt Ramsey sind wahre Zuschauermagneten. Es gibt zwei Pubs (The Central und The Swan) direkt an der Strecke und viele Läden, Fish&Chips-Stände und andere Snackbuden in der Nähe. Die Fahrer müssen stark bremsen, um eine steile Rechtskurve am Eingang zum Platz und eine sanfte Linksbiegung am Ausgang zu durchfahren. Zuschauer können sich vor das Rathaus stellen oder den beschränkten Platz am Ende einer Nebenstraße, die vom Platz wegführt, verwenden. Von Seitenstraßen zu beiden Seiten der Strecke hat man Blick auf den Ausgang auf eine kurze Gerade.

◀ P ✕ WC 👁 Die niedrigen Geschwindigkeiten erleichtern das Fotografieren. Zoomt man nicht zu nah an die Fahrer heran, kann man im Hintergrund die einzigartige TT-Atmosphäre einfangen.

Cruikshanks

Eine tückische ansteigende Rechtskurve führt auf die holprige Straße May Hill. Sie wird mit bis zu 190 km/h durchfahren. Man hat von beiden Seiten der Straße gute Sicht auf die Kurve und in der Nähe gibt es eine Fußgängerbrücke. Sie können auch vom Hügel aus zuschauen. Hier gibt es auf beiden Seiten der Strecke Öffnungen, die über Nebenstraßen zugänglich sind. In der Nähe der A18 von Ramsey nach Douglas und dem

Bahnhof des Manx Electric Railway. ◀ P

Ramsey Hairpin

Sehr langsame Haarnadelkurve unter Bäumen, an der sich die zweite Kommentatorenkabine von Manx Radio befindet. Es gibt begrenzten Platz zum Zuschauen und das Parken in der Nähe kann sich schwierig gestalten. Zugang von der A18 über eine Straße links neben dem MER-Bahnübergang in Ballure. ◀

Der Bergabschnitt

Bei schönem Wetter ist die A16, die Ramsey verlässt und die unbewohnte Berglandschaft durchquert, ehe sie hinab nach Douglas führt, besonders malerisch. Es gibt hier zahlreiche sowohl leicht zugängliche als auch abgelegene Aussichtspunkte.

The Gooseneck

Hierbei handelt es sich um eine steile Rechtskurve, die sich auf dem Anstieg hinter Ramsey befindet und bei gutem Wetter eine tolle Aussicht auf das Meer bietet. Hier sieht man die Fahrer schon aus großer Entfernung herannahen, außerdem kann man beobachten, wie sie bremsen und in die Kurve fahren. Zugang bei gesperrten Straßen über den schmalen Weg D28, ab einem leicht zu übersehenden Abzweig der A2 an der Hibernia-Kreuzung. Gegen eine Gebühr kann auf einem Feld geparkt werden. Für Motorräder gibt es begrenzte Parkmöglichkeiten in der Straße.

◀ ☰ P WC 👁 Gute Möglichkeiten zum Fotografieren und Filmen.

The Bungalow

Lange Kurven mit Bahnübergang und langer Sicht in beide Richtungen sowie Fußgängerbrücke. Folgen Sie von hier aus der malerischen A14 nach Sulby Glen oder Ginger Hall innerhalb der Strecke. Sie können auch von Laxey mit dem Snaefell Mountain Railway anreisen. Mit dieser Bahn erreichen Sie auch das Café auf dem Gipfel.

◀ ☰ P WC

Von hier aus können Sie auch entlang der Strecke wandern, achten Sie aber auf weiche Stellen im Hochmoor.

👁 Es sind viele verschiedene Winkel möglich, dazu gehören landschaftlich sehr schöne Aufnahmen von außerhalb der Strecke über die Kurven in Richtung Brandywell.

Brandywell

Diese Linksbiegung wird mit 160 km/h und schneller durchfahren. Hier, dicht bei Hailwood Heights – dem höchsten Punkt der Strecke – heben sich die wahren Meister des Gebirges vom Rest ab. Bei schlechtem Wetter gibt es keine Möglichkeiten zum Unterstellen, Erfrischungen nicht garantiert, keine Toiletten. Parken ist an der B10 möglich, die auf einer schönen Strecke nach Barregarrow und Douglas (über Injebreck) und über eine einspurige asphaltierte Moorstraße nach Ballaugh Bridge führt. ⇆ ⚏ P

Keppel Gate/Kate's Cottage

Am eigentlichen Anfang der Bergabfahrt befindet sich eine Linkskurve, nach der die Straße zu einem kaum einsehbaren Linksknick an dem einsamen Häuschen führt. Hier werden Geschwindigkeiten über 160 km/h erreicht. Durch Quellwasser ist die Straße auf der Ideallinie oft feucht.

Im oberen Bereich kann man gut und weit sehen, die Böschung gegenüber dem Häuschen ist zu Fuß über einen schmalen 750 m langen Weg ab Creg-ny-Baa erreichbar.

Nach einer deutlich längeren Wanderung die Strecke entlang erreichen Sie die Linksbiegungen beim 33. Meilenstein, die Linkskurve namens Windy Corner und drei schnelle Linksknicke bei Duke's.

⇆ P 👁 Viele interessante Blickwinkel. Achten Sie darauf, keine gesperrten Bereiche zu betreten.

Creg-ny-Baa

Ein Pub/Restaurant lockt zahlreiche Zuschauer zu der mit ca. 130 km/h befahrenen Linkskurve, von der aus Sie einen guten Blick zu der von Kate's Cottage hinab verlaufenden welligen Gerade haben. Es gibt am Eingang der Kurve zwei große Tribünen, ein privates Unternehmen (geringe Gebühr). Am Ausgang der Kurve befindet sich eine Fanzone mit 400 Sitzplätzen. Bei gesperrten Straßen Zugang über die B12, die die A2 etwa einen Kilometer außerhalb von Onchan kreuzt.

⇆ ✕ P WC 👁 Die besten Stellen sind außerhalb der Strecke mit Blick zurück zu Kate's Cottage zu finden.

John McGuinness, Parliament Square, TT Zero

Le TT et le Festival de Moto de lÎle de Man

Le tour de 37,73 miles de la Mountain Course offre de nombreux endroits pour suivre le spectacle tant et si bien qu'il est difficile de savoir où aller.

Les visiteurs réguliers du TT ont souvent des lieux de prédilection, tandis qu'il est recommandé aux nouveaux venus d'essayer d'aller vers différents lieux de manière à obtenir un avant-goût le plus complet possible de l'atmosphère pendant leur séjour. Vous ne pouvez pas parcourir l'ensemble du circuit en un seul TT. Toutefois, il est possible de passer d'un point de vue à un autre lorsque les routes sont fermées, et ceux qui ont le privilège de se trouver sur l'île lors des entraînements peuvent essayer plusieurs endroits. Et il y a toujours une prochaine fois, bien sûr !

Vérifiez les horaires de fermeture des routes et notez que les premiers arrivés sur les sites d'observation gratuits appréciés du public sont les premiers servis. Où que vous soyez, on peut vous demander de faire un don visant à couvrir les coûts du service d'ambulance aérien par hélicoptère ou pour tout autre organisme.

Tenez compte des panneaux à valeur légale signalisant les zones d'accès réglementé ou interdit imposées uniquement dans l'intérêt de la sécurité des pilotes et des spectateurs. Soyez toujours conscients que lorsque des machines pesant plus de 200 kg et filant à des vitesses approchant les 200 mph, la probabilité d'un accident doit être prise au sérieux. Respectez les propriétés privées et les terres agricoles, ne laissez jamais tomber quelque chose sur la route, ne donnez pas à manger aux mouettes et veuillez ne jeter aucun détritus. Il est plus simple de trouver à se garer en moto qu'en voiture. Toutefois, prenez garde à ne pas provoquer un embouteillage.

Les nombreuses routes champêtres surprenantes de l'île donnent accès à plusieurs tronçons de la course lorsque les routes sont fermées pour l'évènement – et procurent du plaisir à les parcourir en moto. Tenez

⚓	**Accès lorsque les rues sont fermées**
🚫	**Aucun accès**
P	**Stationnement**
WC	**Toilettes**
☕	**Collations et boissons**
✕	**Déjeuner**
📷	**Photographie tip**

compte du fait que vous vous trouvez à l'extérieur de la boucle fermée ou à l'intérieur et que votre libre circulation est clairement limitée. Une route de liaison entre Quarterbridge et Braddan passe en dessous du circuit, mais elle est étroite et congestionnée par les voitures pendant les courses. Il est possible de traverser le circuit à pied en passant les ponts situés à Douglas, Ramsey et au Bungalow. Les véhicules peuvent passer plusieurs intersections entre les courses.

Pour le June TT, vous pouvez acheter un billet Fanzone ticket pour accéder à la tribune sur la Glencrutchery Road et à deux autres tribunes autour du circuit. Il est recommandé de réserver plusieurs mois à l'avance.

Pour suivre la course et rester informé de la fermeture des routes, écoutez la Manx Radio TT (sur 1368AM dans toute l'île, sur 87.9FM à Douglas et sur 100.6FM dans le nord de l'île) à la radio ou sur un smartphone ou une tablette à large bande. Manx Radio TT possède également une page Facebook. Les courses peuvent être suivies en direct sur www.iomtt.com à partir de l'endroit où vous pouvez télécharger l'application TT extrêmement utile.

AUX ALENTOURS DE DOUGLAS
La Grandstand, Glencrutchery Road
La Grandstand pouvant accueillir 1000 personnes ne semble pas être le meilleur endroit pour voir les motos en action mais vous pouvez être certains d'avoir une excellente vue du départ, des arrêts de ravitaillement, des pilotes prenant le drapeau à damiers et du podium de cérémonie des trois premiers finalistes. Partout on entend des commentaires, bien qu'il soit utile d'avoir des jumelles pour suivre la progression des pilotes sur le très vieux tableau d'affichage géré par des Boy Scouts et Cubs. Errez dans le village TT derrière la tribune et jouissez

de l'atmosphère festive, des établissements gastronomiques, du chapiteau abritant un bar et de la zone marchande.

Il est recommandé de réserver assez tôt ses tickets pour la tribune principale, mais s'ils ne sont pas tous vendus, certains pourront être achetés dans un kiosque les jours de course. Une tribune pouvant accueillir 300 détenteurs de billets à Nobles Park donne sur la ligne où les coureurs à l'arrivée retournent au paddock, ainsi que sur le circuit. ⊷ P ✕ wc ⊙ permet d'être près des pilotes et des machines.

Pour un forfait d'accueil complet avec un accès privilégié aux pilotes et informations sur les jours de courses, les billets VIP peuvent être réservés à l'avance pour un peu plus de £300.

Hillberry et Cronk-ny-Mona

Regardez approcher les pilotes à grande vitesse du virage Brandish à 3/4 miles (un kilomètre) et délectez-vous de la prise du virage Hillberry à droite à 150 mph, en essayant de ne pas emprunter la sortie trop large. Une tribune payante se trouve à l'extérieur du circuit avec des équipements sanitaires de base. Une route de campagne relie Hilberry à la School Road, Onchan qui est sur la route principale A2.

Cronk-ny-Mona est une courbe à gauche rapide, qu'il est possible de voir uniquement à l'extérieur du circuit où une intersection de la A21 et de la route secondaire mène à des liaisons vers plusieurs points de vue différents le long des premiers miles (kilomètres du tour) via le réseau routier à l'intérieur du circuit.

⊷ P sur une route de campagne étroite, soyez prêts à marcher. ⊙ pan à partir du virage extérieur.

Signpost Corner et Bedstead Corner

Un rond-point quand les routes sont ouvertes, Signpost est un virage à droite relativement lent (80 mph/129 km/h) tout droit sorti d'une crête sans visibilité et suivi du virage à gauche bedstead. Une maison privée donnant sur le Signalpost est ouverte au public qui peut faire un don au Fonds d'hélicoptères. ⊷ Par l'A39 à partir de l'intersection de l'A18 au Manx Arms pub à Onchan. ⚑ P wc ⊙ pan à partir du virage extérieur.

Governor's Bridge

Une épingle à cheveux à droite difficile très lente suivie par une courbe vers la gauche serpente entre le Governor's Dip ombragée et une sortie ascendante à droite sur la Glencrutchery Road. La route principale A18 menant à Onchan et la B34 sont toujours bondées

James Hillier, Start line, TT

pour voir l'épingle à cheveux. Aucun spectateur dans le Dip, mais l'intersection de la Victoria Road offre un bon panorama sur les pilotes accélérant dans le dernier virage avant la ligne d'arrivée. 🏍 P

Croisements de St Ninian

Les pneus rasent le bitume quand les motos virent à gauche au croisement et s'engagent dans la descente Bray Hill à 170 mph. Il se peut que les places debout avec vue imprenable soient serrées, mais il est facile de s'y rendre depuis le centre ville de Douglas. Elles offrent les commodités d'une passerelle et d'une station d'information avec un magasin. 🏍 ✕ P

Bray Hill

Époustouflant! Les machines dévalent les pentes à 180 mph ou plus pour s'embarquer vers la gauche à travers le raccordement à cinq voies en bas alors que la suspension est complètement écrasée. Une zone gratuite avec un panorama imprenable au pied de la colline juste à côté de la Stonex Road se remplit rapidement. Une tribune se trouve en face de la route offrant un panorama gratuit depuis les bouts des Thorney Road, Cronkbourne Road situées à l'extérieur du circuit et de la Tromode Road à l'intérieur.

Plus en hauteur, vous pouvez regarder depuis des routes secondaires situées à l'extérieur du circuit, mais elles ne permettent pas de voir bien loin. Plus loin, il existe un espace limité sur une propriété privée offrant une vue sur le cabrage des coureurs le long de la Quarterbridge Road alors qu'ils sortent du creux au pied de la colline. Demandez une autorisation et arrivez très tôt. 🏍 ♨ WC P mais pas très prêt du circuit. 👁 difficile d'obtenir de bonnes photos à partir des zones du public sans un équipement professionnel.

Quarterbridge

Les pilotes doivent freiner brusquement à l'entrée de ce virage très serré à droite, le premier que l'on peut réellement appeler virage depuis le départ et un rond-point sur des routes ouvertes. Vous vous rapprochez de l'action le long du Quaterbridge Pub hospitalier, mais vous devez regarder à travers de hautes clôtures de protection grillagées. Il existe également des espaces pour spectateurs l'autre côté de la route, au bâtiment à toit plat blanc. L'accès aux routes fermées et les places de

stationnement ne sont pas un problème. 🏍 ✕ WC P

Braddan Bridge

Un virage serré à droite en franchissant le pont est suivi d'une courbe à gauche et d'une boucle vers la droite. Choisissez deux sites payants distincts pour assister au spectacle à l'extérieur du circuit. Les gradins d'environ 400 places donnent sur les courbes principales, tandis que les terrains de l'église de Bradden avec un nombre de place plus limité donnent sur la boucle vers la gauche où les pilotes accélèrent à fond. Les deux sites disposent de restaurants et de toilettes, bien que l'église soit également réputée pour sa cuisine familiale au sein de sa salle paroissiale et pour ses commodités permanentes accessibles aux personnes handicapées et avec un espace change bébé.

Les terrains de la Old Church abritent un point de vue gratuit dont l'espace est limité. 🏍 ✕ P

UNION MILLS À ST JOHN'S
Union Mills

Le sympathique Railway Inn, situé à l'extérieur du circuit juste à côté de la route secondaire B32 Lhergy Cripperty, donne sur la courbe à droite quand il dévale vers la gauche dans le village. La brasserie avec terrasse en plein air récemment agrandie offre un bon point de vue.

Pour changer, allez voir les pilotes s'engager dans la courbe à gauche rapide à 120 mph à partir des terrains de la Church Hall où des collations sont servies, ou le Memorial Hall situé à côté du carrefour Strang Road à l'extérieur de la course. Un dépanneur se trouve à l'intersection qui ferme lors du racing. 🏍 ✕ P nous vous conseillons de venir tôt. 👁 Des photos exceptionnelles peuvent être prises, notamment avec un objectif longue distance.

Ligne droite de Ballahutchin

Les spectateurs passionnés trouveront à se placer à l'extérieur du circuit, respecter les zones réglementées. 🚫

Crosby

Un trajet à toute berzingue à 180 mph et plus à travers le village avec vue à partir d'intersections avec la B35 (extérieur de la course) ou l'A23 (intérieur). Si vous cherchez confort et commodités, le Crosby Hotel pub qui possède une aire de stationnement reste le meilleur choix, notez toutefois qu'il n'y a ni entrée ni sortie tant que les routes sont fermées. ⃠ ✕ P wc

Le Highlander

Les motos peuvent être poussées à 200 mph sur cette ligne droite descendante passant devant le restaurant Highlander qui possède une aire de stationnement de l'autre côté de la route.

Des collations ainsi que des repas peuvent y être pris, notez toutefois qu'il n'y a ni entrée ni sortie tant que les routes sont fermées. ⃠ ✕ P wc

Le Hawthorn

Le pub gastronomique possède une salle pour spectateurs le long de sa façade, de laquelle vous pouvez voir le passage au rapport supérieur des pilotes lorsqu'ils accélèrent avant de négocier le virage à gauche du Greeba Bridge. ⃠ ✕ P wc

Knock Breck Farm, Greeba

Le propriétaire très hospitalier de cette propriété devant laquelle les pilotes passent à plus de 160 mph, non seulement autorise l'accès au jardin de devant et à la basse-cour mais offre également des collations faites maison. Veuillez respecter l'hospitalité.

🡒 par une piste de l'A3 un demi mile au sud de Ballacraine, en passant devant le centre équestre de Kennaa. ✕ P wc

Ballacraine

Un virage serré à droite à côté de St John's où les spectateurs peuvent voir à l'extérieur du circuit à l'intersection de l'A3, ou pour une meilleure vue sur le talus juste à côté de la route. 👁 Bonnes chances de photos.

Dans le village, à proximité de St John's se trouvent un magasin, un pub et un café/restaurant agréé et une petite zone commerciale à proximité de Tynwald Mills abritant deux cafés. 🡒 ✕ P

GLEN HELEN À BALLAUGH

Glen Helen

L'aire de stationnement spacieuse du pub Glen Helen pub donne une vue sur un virage à gauche à 110 mph où la route en lacets qui passe à travers la vallée commence la course avec une montée sèche.

Il y a aussi le restaurant du Swiss Chalet qui, à l'instar du pub, propose généralement un barbecue

pendant les courses. Une tribune élevée à l'extérieur du virage où se trouve une cabine de commentateurs de la Manx Radio offre un spectacle gratuit.

Les aventureux peuvent marcher hors route à l'intérieur du circuit à l'arrière en direction de Black Dub où quelques stationnements sont également disponibles. Tenez compte des zones interdites.

⃠ wc ✕ P 👁 prise de vue de la tribune élevée à proximité de la cabine de commentateurs à Glen Helen pour un angle inhabituel.

Cronk-y-Voddy

Une ligne droite vallonnée où l'on atteint une vitesse de pointe avant d'emprunter une boucle à gauche après le carrefour : suivez la manière dont les meilleurs pilotes relâchent moins que les autres. 🡒 par des chemins étroits sur les deux côtés du circuit. ✕ P à coûts modiques. wc

Barregarrow

Dangereux : Espace limité pour spectateurs au sommet de la colline où des routes secondaires donnent accès.
🡒 au sommet, du côté intérieur du circuit. 🍺

Kirk Michael

Le circuit débute dans le village au Douglas Road Corner où vous pouvez regarder l'intersection A4 à l'extérieur. Plus loin, le Mitre pub situé à l'extérieur donne sur la sortie où les pilotes accélèrent dans l'étroite rue secondaire. ⃠ ✕ wc

En contrebas du village, vous pouvez voir les machines s'élancer vers vous à environ 180 mph depuis une petite aire payante pour spectateurs au Whitehouse Park.

⃠ ✕ P wc 👁 possibilités depuis une tribune à l'extérieur du Douglas Road corner. Pour un plein d'action époustouflant dans les rues du village, garez-

> **Les jours pendant lesquels aucune course n'est programmée, une multitude d'évènements a lieu partout sur l'île à Ramsey, Laxey, Peel et Port Erin. Le mardi de la semaine de course a lieu (si le temps le permet) le célèbre sprint de Ramsey – un évènement à pleine vitesse sur 1/8 miles. Nous conseillons aux lecteurs d'écouter la Manx Radio ou la Radio TT pour recevoir plus d'informations sur ces évènements et autres, ou de regarder la représentation officielle du TT website www.iomtt.com**

■ ■

vous sur le terrain de camping Glen Wyllin et prenez le sentier le long de l'ancienne voie ferrée pour atteindre la Station Road ou, via un escalier, Bayr ny Balleira. Les deux jouxtent le circuit où vous pouvez rester derrière des barrières. Des objectifs longues distances sont nécessaires pour avoir de meilleurs résultats.

Rhencullen

Spectateurs limités sur cette portion terrifiante pour ses rotations et relèvements de roues. Accès par chemins via Orrisdale de l'extérieur du circuit. Obéissez aux instructions du service d'ordre.

🏍 ♨ P à coûts modiques.

Ballaugh Bridge

Chacun devrait y venir au moins une fois pour regarder les coureurs bondirent sur le célèbre pont à dos-d'âne. Vous pouvez apercevoir plus de choses derrière les barrières à l'extérieur du circuit et avoir accès à un dépanneur.

🏍 extérieur du circuit par des routes secondaires menant à des points de vue à Sulby ainsi que par des routes menant à Ramsey et Douglas.

🏍 intérieur du circuit à Brandywell, Barregarrow par des routes de montagne pittoresques, accès aux sites de Douglas/Union Mills via Injebreck.
✕ P wc

Le Raven Inn convivial situé l'autre côté de la route est extrêmement attrayant. 🚫 ✕ P wc 👁 arrivez tôt pour trouver

une place derrière la barrière en face du pub. S'il y a trop de monde, vous pourriez avoir besoin d'une boîte ou d'un marchepied pour avoir une vue dégagée.

Ballacrye

Virage à droite ultra-rapide et une crête qui soulève la roue avant. Une tribune accueille ici 200 détenteurs de billets Franzone uniquement. 🚫 ♨ wc

SULBY À RAMSEY
Sulby Glen

L'accueillant Sulby Glen pub se trouve à l'extérieur du circuit à un carrefour sur le départ cahoteux de la ligne droite Sulby Straight ultra-rapide où les pilotes les plus rapides atteignent les 190mph. Vous pouvez également regarder à partir des barrières sur la route A14 qui croise la ligne droite, et un magasin vendant de légères collations se trouve à l'intérieur du circuit où l'A14 communique avec Ginger Hall et le Bungalow. A l'extérieur du circuit, elle fait le lien avec le Sulby Bridge et le réseau routier du nord de l'île. 🏍 Des véhicules peuvent traverser sous directives pendant les intervalles entre les courses. ✕ P wc

Sulby Bridge

Un freinage brusque est nécessaire pour stopper la vitesse terrifiante acquise sur la ligne droite de manière à contourner le virage serré à droite. Une tribune payante (pas une Fanzone) et quelques espaces pour

Jamie Hamilton, Ballaugh Bridge, TT

spectateurs se trouvent à l'extérieur du circuit en amont du virage et qui partent de la barrière au carrefour routier situé sur l'A17. 👁 perspectives extraordinaires pour des photos avec un impact fort. Prise de vue de la barrière en amont du pont tournée vers le Sulby village.

🚗 ⚡ P WC

Ginger Hall
Un virage à droite pris à près de 120 mph avec l'agréable Ginger Hall pub à l'extérieur où une route secondaire reliant Sulby Glen au The Bungalow rejoint le circuit. Vue de l'extérieur du pub ou à travers les fenêtres, et un stationnement est disponible sur le parking du pub ou sur la route secondaire.

🚗 ✕ P WC 👁 Des motos se trouvent à proximité de la bordure de trottoir droite avant de s'embarder au sommet, permettant aux photographes de prendre de bonnes photos de différents lieux à côté du pub.

Churchtown, Lezayre
Un trajet rapide très spectaculaire avec une bonne vue d'une zone connue sous le nom de « conker trees » (marronniers) à l'intérieur du circuit. Il donne sur une bordure de trottoir saillante présentant une lettre K peinte sur un arbre qui avertit les pilotes. Une route en boucle passant devant la Lezayre Church peut faire lieu d'aire de stationnement. Aucun accès lorsque les routes sont fermées.

🚫 ⚡ P near church. WC

👁 Les photographes avec un laissez-passer de presse ne sont pas privilégiés ici ! Vous aurez besoin d'un téléobjectif court/moyen et une vitesse d'obturation rapide. Avec rien d'autre qu'un réflex numérique professionnel standard, vous avez besoin de mettre au point manuellement en utilisant un endroit sur la route que les motos traversent, puis d'appuyer sur le bouton un instant avant qu'elles passent devant.

Si vous vous trouvez dans le nord de l'île, n'oubliez pas les thés TT sont servis depuis 1993. Ils sont disposés dans la salle paroissiale du village de Bride par les dames de la paroisse.

AIRE DE RAMSEY
Parliament Square
Situés dans la ville de Ramsey, ces virages rapides attirent les foules. Il existe deux pubs, le Central et le Swan, à droite sur le parcours ainsi que de nombreux magasins, restaurants de fish & chip et autres établissements gastronomiques à proximité. Les pilotes doivent freiner brusquement pour négocier un virage serré à droite dans le square et légèrement à gauche à la sortie. Les spectateurs peuvent se tenir en face de l'hôtel de ville ou utiliser un espace limité à l'extrémité d'une ruelle menant au square. Les routes secondaires de part et autre donnent une vue de la sortie sur la courte ligne droite.

🚗 P ✕ WC 👁 Les faibles vitesses facilitent le travail des photographes. Si vous ne zoomez pas de près, les fonds créent une atmosphère unique.

Cruikshanks
Une montée traîtresse à droite menant à May Hill cahoteuse, prise jusqu'à 120 mph. Bonnes vues de la courbe des deux côtés de la route avec une passerelle toute proche. Vous pouvez également regarder sur la côte depuis les ouvertures latérales de part et d'autre du circuit accessible par des ruelles. Tout près de l'A18 menant de Ramsey à Douglas et gare du Manx Electric Railway. 🚗 P

Ramsey Hairpin
Épingle à cheveux très lente à l'ombre des arbres négligée par le deuxième point de commentaire de la Manx Radio. L'espace limité pour les spectateurs et un stationnement à proximité peuvent être un problème. Accès de l'A18 par une petite route à côté à gauche du passage du tramway Ballure MER. 🚗

Le tronçon montagneux
Splendide par beau temps, la route A16 qui monte de Ramsey et traverse les régions montagneuses inhabitées avant de descendre vers Douglas offre de nombreux points de vue, tous facilement accessibles et isolés.

Le Gooseneck
Un crochet serré à droit comme le nom l'indique en montée de Ramsey avec des vues magnifiques sur la mer par beau temps. Il est possible de voir l'approche des pilotes à une certaine distance freinant brusquement et avec un comportement exceptionnel dans les virages. Route fermée accessible par la voie étroite D28 menant à l'intersection facile à manquer sur l'A2 à Hibernian. Parking payant dans un champ, plusieurs stationnements gratuits pour les motos en ligne.

🚗 ⚡ P WC 👁 bonnes perspectives pour des photos ou vidéos.

■ ■

Le Bungalow

Larges courbes avec un passage de ligne de tramway et panorama dans les deux directions et passerelle. Prenez la route pittoresque A14 à partir d'ici pour atteindre Sulby Glen ou Ginger Hall à l'intérieur du circuit. Ou venez au Snaefell Mountain Railway de Laxey, que vous pouvez également prendre pour déguster un café au sommet. 🚗 🚻 P WC

Il est possible de marcher aux abords du circuit en partant d'ici, mais faites attention aux tourbières molles. 👁 Nombreux angles différents possibles dont des photos vraiment panoramiques de l'extérieur du circuit au-delà des virages vers Brandywell.

Brandywell

Ce crochet à gauche pris à plus de 100 mph différencie les maîtres de la montagne des autres, juste au-delà des hauteurs de Hailwood, le point culminant du circuit. Exposé au mauvais temps, collations non garanties, pas de toilettes. Stationnement le long de la route B10 qui relie Barregarrow à Douglas (via Injebreck) sur des routes étroites et à Ballaugh Bridge via une route dans les lands goudronnée à voie unique. 🚗 🚻 P

Keppel Gate/Kate's Cottage

Là où la descente de la montagne commence réellement, avec un crochet à gauche suivi de la descente vers une boucle à gauche prise à plus de 100 mph sans visibilité en passant devant le cottage. De l'eau de source mouille souvent la route du circuit.

De bons panoramas peuvent être atteints du tronçon en amont et la tribune située en face du cottage est accessible à pied 1/2 miles (750 m) par un chemin étroit partant de Creg-ny-Baa.

En marchant plus longtemps le long du circuit, vous pourrez voir les courbes à gauche à la 33ème étape, le Windy Corner pris à gauche et trois boucles à gauche très rapides à Duke's. 🚗 P 👁 Nombreux angles intéressants, veillez à rester dans les zones admises.

Creg-ny-Baa

Un restaurant/pub attire les foules venues pour le crochet à gauche pris à 80 mph avec une vue exceptionnelle sur la ligne droite cahoteuse descendant de Kate's. Il y a deux tribunes, un secteur privé (somme modique) donnant sur l'entrée de la courbe et une Fanzone de 400 places à la sortie. Accès aux routes fermées via la B12 qui croise l'A2 à quelques 3/4 miles (1 kilomètre) après Onchan.

🚗 ✕ P WC 👁 Les meilleures places se trouvent à l'extérieur à l'approche du virage en regardant vers Kate's.

Alan Oversby, Creg-ny-Baa, Classic TT

El TT y el Isle of Man Festival of Motorcycling

El circuito de la montaña (Mountain Course), con sus 37,73 millas, ofrece tantos puntos para seguir la carrera que resulta complicado decantarse por alguno.

Los habituales del TT tienen normalmente sus lugares predilectos, mientras que en el caso de los que visitan la isla por primera vez, se recomienda que prueben diferentes emplazamientos durante su estancia para imbuirse todo lo posible de este singular ambiente. Resulta imposible abarcar todo el circuito en un TT, pero sí se puede cambiar de unos puntos a otros mientras las carreteras permanecen cerradas para que los afortunados que se encuentran en la isla durante los entrenamientos puedan probar un mayor número de lugares. Y, por supuesto, seguro que hay una próxima ocasión.

Compruebe los horarios de cierre de carreteras y tenga presente que los puntos de seguimiento gratuitos más populares, que se van ocupando por orden de llegada del público, se llenan muy rápido. Cualquiera que sea el punto en el que se encuentre, se le pedirá que colabore con un donativo para sufragar los gastos del helicóptero ambulancia o de cualquier otra importante obra benéfica del TT.

Respete las señales obligatorias que indican zonas restringidas o prohibidas; estas zonas se establecen pensando en la seguridad de los pilotos y espectadores. Tenga siempre presente que las motos pesan más de 200 kg y circulan a velocidades próximas a las 200 mi/h, por lo que no es asunto baladí la posibilidad de que se produzca un incidente. Respete la propiedad privada y las tierras de cultivo; no tire objetos a la carretera, absténgase de alimentar a las gaviotas y no tire desperdicios al suelo. Resulta más sencillo encontrar aparcamiento si se desplaza en moto y no en coche; procure no obstruir el tráfico.

La isla cuenta con un llamativo número de

⟿	**Acceso con carreteras cerradas**
⊘	**Sin acceso**
P	**Aparcamiento**
WC	**Aseos**
⚌	**Aperitivos y bebidas**
✕	**Comidas**
👁	**Consejo fotográfico**

carreteras secundarias para acceder a muchos puntos del circuito cuando las vías principales están cerradas por la competición; además, son motivo de disfrute si las recorre en moto. Tenga siempre presente si se encuentra en el exterior del anillo cerrado o en el interior del mismo, dadas las obvias restricciones a la circulación que encontrará en este último. Existe una vía de enlace entre Quarterbridge y Braddan que discurre bajo el circuito, pero es estrecha y está congestionada de coches durante las carreras. Es posible cruzar el circuito caminando por los puentes sitos en Douglas, Ramsey y Bungalow. En algunos cruces los vehículos tienen permiso para circular entre carreras.

Para el TT de junio puede adquirir un billete Fanzone que le permitirá acceder a la tribuna principal de Glencrutchery Road y a otras dos gradas a lo largo del trazado. Se recomienda realizar la reserva con varios meses de antelación.

Para seguir las carreras y mantenerse informado sobre los cortes de carreteras, sintonice Manx Radio TT (1368 AM en toda la isla, 87.9 FM en Douglas y 100.6 FM en la zona norte) vía radio o por banda ancha en su smartphone o tableta. Manx Radio TT cuenta además con página en Facebook. Pueden consultarse en directo los tiempos de carrera en www.iomtt.com, donde además está disponible para descarga la utilísima aplicación TT App.

CERCANÍAS DE DOUGLAS
Grandstand, Glencrutchery Road
Puede que la tribuna principal de pago con 1000 asientos no sea el mejor lugar para disfrutar de la acción, pero sí tendrá garantizadas unas magníficas vistas de la línea de salida, las paradas para repostar, las banderas a cuadros y las ceremonias de entrega de premios a los tres primeros clasificados. Existe un servicio de comentarios por megafonía que se escucha por toda la tribuna; el uso de prismáticos resulta útil

para consultar las evoluciones de los pilotos en el antiguo tablero marcador actualizado por integrantes de los boy scouts y cubs. Recorra el TT Village detrás de la tribuna y disfrute de la atmósfera festiva visitando los puestos de comida, la carpa con el bar y la zona dedicada a productos de merchandising.

Se recomienda reservar con antelación las entradas a la tribuna principal; si no están agotadas, las podrá adquirir en el puesto de venta habilitado los días de carreras. La tribuna de pago con 300 asientos de Nobles Park tiene vistas al circuito y a la vía por la que los pilotos regresan al paddock. ➔ P ✕ wc ☞ una oportunidad para estar cerca de los pilotos y de sus máquinas.

Por un precio ligeramente superior a 300 £ pueden adquirirse billetes de zona VIP, paquetes completos con acceso privilegiado a los pilotos e información los días de carreras.

Hillberry y Cronk-ny-Mona

Disfrute viendo a los pilotos descender tres cuartos de milla (un kilómetro) a gran velocidad desde Brandish Corner para enfilar a 150 mi/h la curva de derechas de Hillberry sin irse demasiado en la salida. En el exterior del circuito hay una tribuna de pago con aseos básicos. Una carretera secundaria enlaza Hillberry con School Road, Onchan, a la salida de la ruta A2.

Cronk-ny-Mona es un viraje de izquierdas a alta velocidad con visión solo en el exterior del circuito; el cruce con la A21 y una vía secundaria permite acceder a numerosos puntos de seguimiento a lo largo de las primeras millas gracias a la red de carreteras internas del circuito. ➔ P prepárese para caminar por la estrecha carretera secundaria. ☞ fotografías desde la esquina exterior.

Signpost Corner y Bedstead Corner

Signpost es una rotonda cuando las carreteras están abiertas al tráfico; se trata de una curva de derechas relativamente lenta (80 mi/h/129 km/h) que se traza justo después de un cambio de rasante ciego y va seguida de la curva de izquierdas de Bedstead. Hay una vivienda particular que da a Signpost a la que puede acceder el público; debe aportarse un donativo para costear el servicio de helicóptero. ➔ Por la A39 desde el cruce con la A18 junto al pub Manx Arms de Onchan. ✕ P wc ☞ fotografías desde la esquina exterior.

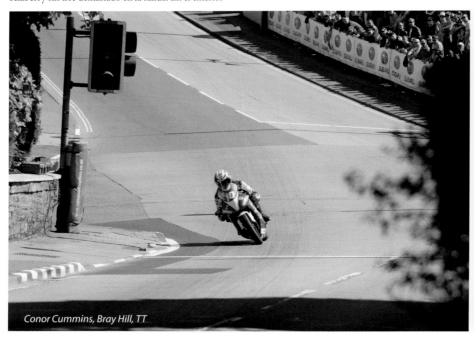

Conor Cummins, Bray Hill, TT

Governor's Bridge

Una horquilla de derechas, muy delicada y lenta, seguida de una curva de izquierdas para enfilar el oscuro Governor's Dip y una salida en subida a la derecha para tomar Glencrutchery Road. Hay sitio para ver esta horquilla desde la A18 dirección a Onchan y desde la secundaria B34. Está prohibido seguir la competición desde el Dip, pero el cruce de Victoria Road ofrece una buena visión de los pilotos acelerando al salir de la última curva antes de la línea de meta. ⊐ P

Cruce de St Ninian's

Los neumáticos se levantan del asfalto al girar las motos a la izquierda en el cruce y enfilar la bajada de Bray Hill a 170 mi/h. Puede resultar complicado encontrar un sitio con buenas vistas; no obstante, es sencillo llegar a este punto desde el centro de Douglas y cuenta con un práctico puente peatonal y una gasolinera con tienda. ⊐ ✕ P

Bray Hill

¡Brutal! Las motos enfilan esta bajada a 180 mi/h o más girando bruscamente a la izquierda en la intersección de cinco calles situada al fondo, donde una salvaje compresión hunde totalmente las suspensiones. La zona de acceso gratuito con excelentes vistas a la falda de la colina junto a Stoney Road se llena rápidamente de aficionados. En el lado opuesto de la carretera hay una grada y puede seguirse la carrera de forma gratuita desde los extremos de Thorney Road y Cronkbourne Road en el exterior del trazado y desde Tromode Road en su interior.

Más arriba puede observarse el espectáculo desde vías laterales en el exterior del trazado, aunque no se obtienen vistas amplias. Más adelante hay espacio limitado en las propiedades privadas para ver a los pilotos rodar por Quarterbridge Road y surgir de la hondonada al pie de la colina. Obtenga permiso y acuda muy temprano. ⊐ ☰ ⓦⓒ P pero no muy cerca del circuito. ⊙ difícil sacar buenas imágenes desde zonas públicas sin un equipo profesional.

Quarterbridge

Los pilotos deben hacer una fuerte frenada en este delicado viraje de derechas, la primera curva propiamente dicha tras la salida y una rotonda cuando las carreteras están abiertas. Puede disfrutar del espectáculo desde el acogedor pub Quarterbridge, pero a través de las altas vallas de protección de malla. Hay también un lugar para espectadores al otro lado de la calle, junto al edificio blanco con cubierta plana. El acceso por carreteras cerradas o el aparcamiento no suponen ningún problema. ⊐ ✕ ⓦⓒ P

Braddan Bridge

Una cerrada curva de derechas en el puente, seguida de otra amplia de izquierdas y un giro de derechas. Para colocarse en el exterior del trazado, opte por alguno de los dos recintos de pago de diferentes propietarios. La grada escalonada para 400 personas da a los principales virajes, mientras que un limitado número de asientos en los jardines de la iglesia de Braddan permiten ver el giro de izquierdas donde los pilotos salen a fondo. Ambos emplazamientos disponen de catering y aseos, si bien la iglesia destaca por su comida casera y sus instalaciones permanentes, incluyendo acceso para discapacitados y servicio de cambio de pañales.

Hay una zona gratuita pero no muy grande en los terrenos de Old Church. ⊐ ✕ P

UNION MILLS A ST JOHN'S
Union Mills

El agradable Railway Inn, situado en el exterior del circuito junto a la secundaria B32 de Lhergy Cripperty va a dar a la curva de derechas del trazado que desciende hacia el giro de izquierdas del pueblo. El jardín se ha ampliado recientemente y ofrece un buen punto de seguimiento.

También puede ver a los pilotos negociando a 120 mi/h esta complicada curva de izquierdas desde los jardines de Church Hall, punto en el que se sirven

Los días sin competición la isla alberga un gran número de eventos en Ramsey, Laxey, Peel y Port Erin.

Si el tiempo lo permite, el martes de la semana de competición se celebra el afamado Ramsey Sprint, una prueba de aceleración en un tramo de vía de 1/8 de milla.

Para mayor información sobre estos eventos y otras pruebas, se recomienda a los lectores que sintonicen Manx Radio o Radio TT o accedan a la página web oficial del TT www.iomtt.com

refrigerios, o desde Memorial Hall, cerca del cruce de Strang Road en el interior del circuito. Hay una tienda de conveniencia junto al cruce que cierra cuando se inician las carreras.

🏍 ✕ P se aconseja llegar temprano. 👁 Aquí pueden sacarse fotografías soberbias, especialmente con objetivo largo.

Recta de Ballahutchin
Los espectadores más avispados encuentran lugares en el exterior del circuito; tenga presente las zonas restringidas. 🚫

Crosby
Un tramo del trazado a través de la localidad que se pasa vertiginosamente a más de 180 mi/h; vistas desde las intersecciones con la B35 (exterior del circuito) o la A23 (interior). La mejor opción en cuanto a confort y comodidad la encontramos en el pub del hotel Crosby, que dispone de zona de aparcamiento; tenga presente que está prohibido entrar o salir una vez cerradas las carreteras. 🚫 ✕ P 🚻

Highlander
Las motos alcanzan las 200 mi/h en este tramo recta en bajada que pasa por el restaurante Highlander, que cuenta con zona de aparcamiento cruzando la calle.

Dispone de todo tipo de servicios de restauración, estando prohibido entrar o salir con las carreteras cerradas. 🚫 ✕ P 🚻

Hawthorn
Pub especializado en restauración con una sala en la fachada para seguir la competición, desde donde puede verse a los pilotos subiendo marchas y acelerando para salir de la curva de izquierdas de Greeba Bridge.
🚫 ✕ P 🚻

Knock Breck Farm, Greeba
El hospitalario propietario de esta granja, por la que pasan los pilotos a más de 160 mi/h, no solo permite el acceso a su jardín delantero y corrales, sino que además ofrece refrigerios caseros. Sea respetuoso con la hospitalidad que se le ofrece.

🏍 por un camino al salir de la A3, a media milla al sur de Ballacraine, pasando el centro ecuestre de Kennaa. ✕ P 🚻

Ballacraine
Una cerrada curva de derechas próxima a St John's en la que los espectadores pueden ver las motos desde el exterior del circuito en la intersección con la A3; para obtener mejores vistas, puede seguirse la competición desde el borde de la carretera.

👁 Buenas oportunidades para sacar fotos.

En la cercana St John's encontrará una tienda, un pub y una cafetería-restaurante con licencia para la venta de alcohol, y la pequeña zona comercial en la también próxima Tynwald Mills cuenta con dos cafeterías.
🏍 ✕ P

GLEN HELEN A BALLAUGH
Glen Helen Corner
El espacioso aparcamiento del pub Glen Helen está situado junto a una curva de izquierdas que se toma a 110 mi/h; la sinuosa carretera que pasa por la cañada inicia aquí un pronunciado ascenso.

Además del pub, que normalmente ofrece barbacoas durante las carreras, encontramos el restaurante Swiss Chalet. Hay una ladera elevada fuera de la curva donde se ubica una de las cabinas de comentaristas de Manx Radio; se pueden ver las carreras de forma gratuita.

Los más intrépidos pueden salir de la carretera caminando en el interior del circuito y retroceder a Black Dub donde también hay aparcamiento. Tenga presente las zonas prohibidas.

🚫 🚻 ✕ P 👁 pueden sacarse fotografías desde la ladera elevada próxima a la cabina de comentaristas de Glen Helen para obtener ángulos poco habituales.

Cronk-y-Voddy
Una recta de relieve ondulado donde se marcan elevadas velocidades antes de trazar una curva de derechas justo después del cruce; aquí comprobará cómo los mejores pilotos cortan gas más suavemente que el resto. 🏍 por vías estrechas a ambos lados del circuito. ✕ P por un precio reducido. 🚻

Barregarrow
De quitar el hipo. Muy poco espacio para espectadores en lo alto de la colina; acceso a través de carreteras secundarias. 🏍 arriba, desde el interior del circuito. 🏁

Kirk Michael

El circuito entra en la localidad por Douglas Road Corner, donde puede seguirse la competición en la intersección de la A4 en el exterior. Un poco más adelante el pub Mitre, en el interior, va a dar a la salida, donde los pilotos aceleran al bajar por la angosta calle principal. ◔ ✕ ⓌⒸ

Adentrándose en el pueblo sentirá cómo se le abalanzan las motos a una velocidad aproximada de 180 mi/h desde una pequeña zona de seguimiento de pago en Whitehouse Park. ◔ ✕ Ⓟ ⓌⒸ ◉ posibilidad de tomar fotos desde un lateral en el exterior de Douglas Road Corner. Para disfrutar de toda la intensidad del motociclismo urbano, aparque en el camping de Glen Wyllin y tome el sendero que discurre junto a la antigua vía de ferrocarril hasta acceder a Station Road, o acceda a Bayr ny Balleira a través de las escaleras. Ambos itinerarios lindan con el circuito y podrá seguir las carreras tras las barreras. Se requieren objetivos largos para conseguir buenas fotografías.

Rhencullen

Poco espacio para seguir las carreras en este tremendo tramo con virajes y rasantes donde los neumáticos despegan del suelo. Acceso a través de caminos por Orrisdale desde el exterior del circuito. Respete las indicaciones de los comisarios. ↩ ⚋ Ⓟ por un precio reducido.

Ballaugh Bridge

Un punto del circuito que todo el mundo debería visitar al menos una vez para ver a los pilotos atacar el salto en este famoso puente. Podrá disfrutar de la acción desde detrás de las barreras en el exterior del circuito; acceso a una tienda de conveniencia.

↩ en el exterior del circuito a través de carreteras secundarias hasta los puntos de seguimiento de Sulby, además de por las rutas que llevan a Ramsey y Douglas.
↩ en el interior del circuito dirección a Brandywell, a Barregarrow por pintorescas vías de montaña; acceso a la zona de Douglas/Union Mills por Injebreck.
✕ Ⓟ ⓌⒸ

El agradable Raven Inn al otro lado de la calle cuenta con obvios atractivos. ◔ ✕ Ⓟ ⓌⒸ ◉ se recomienda llegar temprano para conseguir sitio detrás de las barreras frente al pub. Si está muy concurrido puede que necesite una caja o una pequeña escalera para disfrutar de una vista despejada.

Ballacrye

Rapidísima curva de izquierdas y cambio de rasante que hace que las ruedas delanteras despeguen del asfalto.

Dispone de una tribuna Fanzone de pago para 200 personas. ◔ ⚋ ⓌⒸ

SULBY A RAMSEY
Sulby Glen

El acogedor pub Sulby Glen está situado en el exterior del circuito en un cruce donde se inicia la rapidísima y bacheada recta de Sulby; los pilotos más veloces alcanzan aproximadamente 190 mi/h. Pueden seguirse las carreras desde las barreras de la A14 que cruza la recta; hay una tienda donde venden refrigerios en el interior del circuito en el punto donde conectan la A14, Ginger Hall y Bungalow. En el exterior del circuito enlaza con Sulby Bridge y la red de carreteras del norte de la isla. ↩ Los vehículos pueden cruzar cuando así se lo indiquen durante los intervalos entre carreras. ✕ Ⓟ ⓌⒸ

Sulby Bridge

Es necesario frenar a fondo para reducir la enorme velocidad alcanzada en la recta previa y trazar la cerrada curva de derechas. Hay una tribuna de pago (no es una Fanzone) y algo de sitio para seguir la competición en el exterior del circuito antes de la curva y desde la barrera en la intersección de la A17.

◉ Espléndidas oportunidades para realizar fotos impactantes. Dispare su cámara desde el seto antes del puente, apuntando en dirección a Sulby. ↩ ⚋ Ⓟ ⓌⒸ

Ginger Hall

Una curva de izquierdas que se toma a aproximadamente 120 mi/h; en el exterior se encuentra el agradable pub Ginger Hall, donde una carretera secundaria que conecta con Sulby Glen y Bungalow enlaza con el circuito. Hay buena visión desde el exterior del pub o incluso a través de los ventanales; se puede estacionar en el aparcamiento del pub o en la vía lateral.

↩ ✕ Ⓟ ⓌⒸ ◉ Las motos pasan a escasa distancia del bordillo derecho antes de dirigirse al ápice de la curva, permitiendo que los fotógrafos tomen buenas instantáneas desde diversos puntos próximos al pub.

Churchtown, Lezayre

Un tramo rápido y ciertamente espectacular con buena visión desde la zona conocida como "conker trees" en el interior del circuito. Va a dar a una cuneta en saliente con la letra K pintada en un árbol que sirve de aviso a los pilotos. Puede utilizarse como aparcamiento un ramal que pasa por la iglesia de Lezayre. No hay acceso cuando se cierran las carreteras. ◇ ⚏ P cerca de la iglesia. [WC]

👁 Los fotógrafos con pases de prensa no cuentan aquí con ninguna ventaja. Necesitará la ayuda de un teleobjetivo corto o medio y una rápida velocidad de obturación. Con cualquier cámara que no sea una réflex digital profesional estándar, necesitará enfocar manualmente tomando como referencia un punto de la vía sobre el que vaya a pasar la moto, para seguidamente pulsar el botón un instante antes de su paso.

Si se encuentra en el norte de la isla, no se pierda los TT Teas que llevan sirviéndose desde 1993. Se celebran en el hall de la iglesia de la localidad de Bride y están a cargo de mujeres de la congregación.

ZONA DE RAMSEY
Parliament Square
Situadas en la localidad de Ramsey, estas curvas lentas atraen a un enorme gentío. En el circuito hay dos pubs, el Central y el Swan, además de numerosas tiendas,

John McGuinness, Conker Trees, 11

restaurantes de "fish and chips" y otros establecimientos de comida en las proximidades. Los pilotos deben frenar a fondo para trazar una cerrada curva de derechas que les lleva a la plaza y a un suave viraje de izquierdas en la salida. Los espectadores pueden seguir las carreras delante del edificio del Ayuntamiento, o bien ocupar el limitado espacio existente al final de una vía trasera que va a dar a la plaza. Las vías laterales a ambos lados ofrecen vistas de la salida de la curva a una corta recta.
🚗 P ✕ [WC] 👁 Las bajas velocidades facilitan el trabajo de los fotógrafos.
Si no acerca demasiado el zoom, captará de fondo el singular ambiente del TT.

Cruikshanks
Una traicionera curva de derechas en subida que lleva a la bacheada May Hill; se toma a velocidades de hasta 120 mi/h. Buenas vistas de la curva desde ambos márgenes; hay un puente peatonal en las proximidades. También puede ver la colina desde las zonas abiertas a ambos lados del circuito a las que se accede a través de vías secundarias. Próxima a la A18 de Ramsey a Douglas y a la estación terminal del tranvía interurbano eléctrico de la Isla de Man. 🚗 P

Ramsey Hairpin
Una horquilla muy lenta bajo los árboles donde se ubica el segundo puesto de comentaristas de Manx Radio. Espacio limitado para espectadores; puede resultar un problema aparcar en las proximidades. Acceso desde la A18 por una vía a la izquierda junto al cruce de tranvías de Ballure del MER (Manx Electric Railway). 🚗

Tramo de la montaña
Soberbio cuando el tiempo acompaña, la A16, que asciende desde Ramsey y atraviesa esta zona montañosa deshabitada antes de descender hacia Douglas, ofrece muchos puntos aislados y de fácil acceso desde donde seguir la competición.

Gooseneck
Una cerrada curva de derechas, tal como su nombre indica ("cuello de ganso"); espléndidas vistas del mar si el clima lo permite en la subida desde Ramsey. Potente frenada y entrada en curva; puede verse a cierta distancia cómo se van aproximando los pilotos. El acceso con carreteras cerradas se realiza por la estrecha pista D28 desde el cruce en Hibernian Road de la A2

(fácil pasarlo de largo). Hay que pagar para aparcar en este terreno; hay algunos lugares gratuitos donde aparcar motos en el camino.

🏍 ⚡ P wc 👁 *excelentes oportunidades para fotos o vídeos.*

Bungalow

Curvas radicales, un cruce de tranvía, amplias vistas en ambas direcciones y un puente peatonal. Coja la pintoresca A14 desde aquí hasta Sulby Glen o Ginger Hall en el interior del circuito. También puede llegar a este punto desde Laxey en el ferrocarril del monte de Snaefell, o cogerlo hasta la cafetería de la cima.

🏍 ⚡ P wc

Desde aquí se puede caminar por el costado del circuito; no obstante, tenga cuidado con las blandas turberas.

👁 *infinidad de ángulos diferentes, incluyendo espectaculares imágenes desde el exterior del circuito pasando las curvas en dirección a Brandywell.*

Brandywell

Esta curva de izquierdas se toma a más de 100 mi/h y distingue a los maestros de la montaña del resto; punto situado después de Hailwood Heights, la cota más elevada del circuito. Zona expuesta con malas condiciones climáticas. No está garantizado el servicio de refrigerios; sin aseos. Aparcamiento a lo largo de la B10, que conecta con Barregarrow y Douglas (vía Injebreck) por carreteras pintorescas y con Ballaugh Bridge a través de una vía asfaltada de un solo carril que discurre por un páramo. 🏍 ⚡ P

Keppel Gate/Kate's Cottage

Aquí comienza realmente el descenso de la montaña, con una curva de izquierdas seguida de un viraje ciego también de izquierdas junto a la aislada casa que se traza a más de 100 mi/h. El agua de los manantiales moja con frecuencia la trazada correcta.

Buenas y amplias vistas desde el tramo superior; puede accederse al lado contrario de la casa ascendiendo a pie media milla (750 m) por un estrecho sendero desde Creg-ny-Baa.

Una caminata más larga a lo largo del circuito nos lleva a las curvas de izquierdas de la milla 33, al viraje también de izquierdas conocido como Windy Corner y a tres rápidos giros en Duke.

🏍 P 👁 *infinidad de ángulos interesantes; recuerde que debe mantenerse en las zonas permitidas.*

Creg-ny-Baa

El pub-restaurante atrae a gran número de aficionados hasta esta curva de izquierdas que se negocia a 80 mi/h; fantásticas vistas de la bacheada recta en bajada desde Kate's Cottage. Hay dos tribunas, un emplazamiento privado (se paga una pequeña cantidad) que permite ver la entrada a la curva y una Fanzone con 400 asientos en la salida. Acceso con carreteras cerradas por la B12, que se cruza con la A2 a aproximadamente _ de milla (un km) pasado Onchan.

🏍 ✕ P wc 👁 *Los mejores sitios están en el exterior, en la aproximación a la curva mirando hacia Kate's Cottage.*

TT Course Crossing Points and Access Corridors

- Douglas, Ballaquayle Road and Ballanard Road
- Douglas, Stoney Road and Tromode Road
- A1, Douglas, Quarterbridge to Braddan School, Saddle Road, Lhergy Cripperty Road, Strang Road, Union Mills
- A1, Crosby Old Church Road, Eyreton Road and Ballavitchel Road
- A3, Barregarrow crossroads, Michael
- A3, Kirk Michael, Douglas Road Corner and the entrance to Faaie-ny-Cabbal
- A3, Station Road and Glen Road, Ballaugh
- A3, Sulby Glen crossroads, Lezayre
- Ramsey, Christian Street and Westbourne Road
- Ramsey, Lheaney Road and Barrule Park
- A18, Onchan and Douglas, Signpost Corner and Bedstead Corner
- Onchan and Douglas, Governor's Road, Victoria Road and Second Avenue
- Crossing Points and Access Corridors, when open, will be under the control of Police Officers.

For details of up to date opening and closing times telephone the road information line.

ROAD INFORMATION LINE:

01624 685888

Kreuzungspunkte und Zugangswege der TT-Strecke

- Douglas, Ballaquayle Road und Ballanard Road
- Douglas, Stoney Road und Tromode Road
- A1, Douglas, Quarterbridge nach Braddan School, Saddle Road, Lhergy Cripperty Road, Strang Road, Union Mills
- A1, Crosby Old Church Road, Eyreton Road und Ballavitchel Road
- A3, Barregarrow-Kreuzung, Michael
- A3, Kirk Michael, Douglas Road Corner und Zufahrt zu Faaie-ny-Cabbal
- A3, Station Road und Glen Road, Ballaugh
- A3, Sulby-Glen-Kreuzung, Lezayre
- Ramsey, Christian Street und Westbourne Road
- Ramsey, Lheaney Road und Barrule Park
- A18, Onchan und Douglas, Signpost Corner und Bedstead Corner
- Onchan und Douglas, Governor's Road, Victoria Road und Second Avenue
- Kreuzungspunkte und Zugangswege werden von Polizisten kontrolliert, wenn sie geöffnet sind.

Um aktuelle Öffnungs- und Sperrzeiten zu erhalten, rufen Sie die Straßenauskunft an.

STRASSENAUSKUNFT:

01624 685888

Points de passage et voies d'accès au circuit TT

- Douglas, Ballaquayle Road et Ballanard Road
- Douglas, Stoney Road et Tromode Road
- A1, Douglas, Quarterbridge en direction de la Braddan School, Saddle Road, Lhergy Cripperty Road, Strang Road, Union Mills
- A1, Crosby Old Church Road, Eyreton Road et Ballavitchel Road
- A3, Croisement Barregarrow, Michael
- A3, Kirk Michael, Douglas Road Corner et l'entrée de Faaie-ny-Cabbal
- A3, Station Road et Glen Road, Ballaugh
- A3, Sulby Glen crossroads, Lezayre
- Ramsey, Christian Street et Westbourne Road

- Ramsey, Lheaney Road et Barrule Park
- A18, Onchan et Douglas, Signpost Corner et Bedstead Corner
- Onchan et Douglas, Governor's Road, Victoria Road et Second Avenue
- Les points de passage & voies d'accès, si ouverts, sont sous la surveillance des officiers de police.

Pour plus de détails sur la date d'ouverture et de fermeture, téléphonez au service d'information routier.

SERVICE D'INFORMATION ROUTIER

01624 685888

Puntos de paso y corredores de acceso del circuito del TT

Puntos de paso y corredores de acceso del circuito del TT

- Douglas, Ballaquayle Road y Ballanard Road.
- Douglas, Stoney Road y Tromode Road.
- A1, Douglas, Quarterbridge a Braddan School, Saddle Road, Lhergy Cripperty Road, Strang Road, Union Mills.
- A1, Crosby Old Church Road, Eyreton Road y Ballavitchel Road.
- A3, cruce de Barregarrow, Michael.
- A3, Kirk Michael, Douglas Road Corner y la entrada a Faaie-ny-Cabbal.
- A3, Station Road y Glen Road, Ballaugh.
- A3, cruce de Sulby Glen, Lezayre.
- Ramsey, Christian Street y Westbourne Road.

- Ramsey, Lheaney Road y Barrule Park.
- A18, Onchan y Douglas, Signpost Corner y Bedstead Corner.
- Onchan y Douglas, Governor's Road, Victoria Road y Second Avenue.
- Los puntos de paso y los corredores de acceso están controlados por agentes de policía cuando están abiertos al tráfico.

Para obtener detalles actualizados sobre las horas de apertura y cierre, póngase en contacto con el teléfono de información de carreteras.

TELÉFONO DE INFORMACIÓN DE CARRETERAS

01624 685888

Billown Circuit

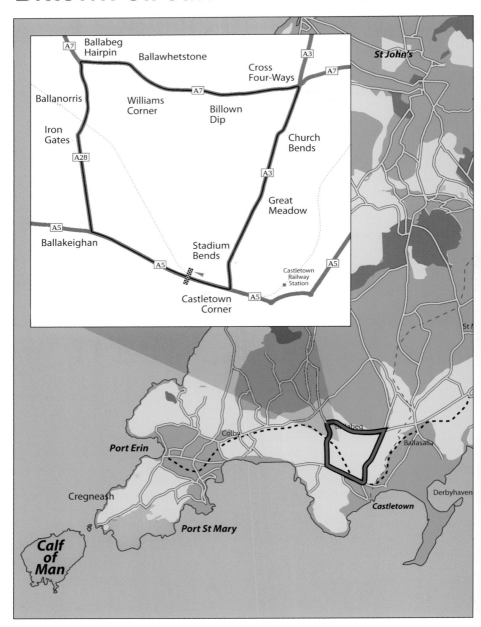

SHUTTER *speed*

A must-have for every fan
of the Isle of Man's
BIG 3 race events

Shutter Speed 2015 Calendar

A collection of images from Dave Collister, a stand-out talent amongst motorsport photographers. Dave's relentless quest for fresh angles and evermore-startling shots from points around the TT Course makes this a stunning addition to the wall of any motorcycle racing enthusiast

A4, opening to 13 A3 portrait spreads £4.95

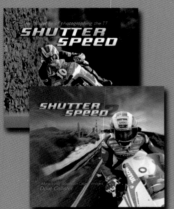

Shutter Speed 2 – More iconic Mountain Course Images

Following on from the success of Shutter Speed – the challenge of photographing the TT, 'Lone Wolf' Dave Collister returns with an all-new collection of iconic Mountain Course images featuring modern-day TT heroes including John McGuiness, Bruce Anstey, 5-wins-in-a-week Ian Hutchinson and the next generation of superstars such as Michael Dunlop and Josh Brookes.

The images are accompanied by fascinating short narratives from the photographer.

220mm x 245mm hardback, 128 pages £10.00

The *Shutter Speed Calendar*, *Shutter Speed* and *Shutter Speed 2* are available from all good book shops on the Isle of Man, or you can order online at: www.lilypublications.co.uk

Lily Publications

Publishers of best selling Isle of Man motorsport, tourism and history books
Lily Publications, PO Box 33, Ramsey, Isle of Man IM99 4LP Tel: +44 (0)1624 898446

The Billown Circuit

Billown may offer less choice of viewing points than the Mountain Course but watching riders on the demanding circuit is always thrilling, especially as the field starts *en masse*. There are none of the day-long road closures that can happen with the bigger circuit, so being stranded at an inaccessible spot without refreshments or conveniences is not such an issue. Money charged for two grandstands, at the start and at Castletown Corner goes towards organising future meetings after hire costs are covered. The Southern 100 Club owns and operates catering outlets at the start/finish, Ballabeg and Cross Four Ways.

Manx Radio covers the racing and there is public address at the start/finish. A live timing app compatible with most up-to-date smart phones will keep you updated on each race, lap-by-lap. Download at www.mylaps.com for a small fee.

Start and finish
A grandstand seating around 200 people overlooks the start/finish line, situated on a straight that starts with a downhill run from Castletown Corner. There is standing room behind barriers on the grassy area between the stand and the race HQ and paddock area, situated where the Arbory Road joins the A5 Castletown Bypass.

A great view of hectic starts and thrilling finishes, a feature of Billown racing, and close to the paddock so you'll see machines up close. 🚗 🚆 P WC 👁 Evening sun adds impact to massed start shots.

Ballakeighan
The right-hand bend at Ballakeighan Farm follows a fast, slightly uphill leftward sweep following the start and finish straight. Can be a real hair-raiser on the first lap as the leading pack comes into view jostling for the best line through. Views from behind walls here and on the approach. 🚗 P 👁 Great for shooting tightly-bunched groups on the first lap.

Iron gates
A half-mile (750m) straight runs gently downhill to the terrifying rightward kink with

Guy Martin, Start, Southern 100

a stone wall and no kerb on the inside.
🚫 👁 For drama, aim to catch bikes grazing inside wall in bend. Or take long views looking back up the straight.

Ballanorris
A sweep to the left past the farm, shaded by trees. A gate to a field on the exit is left open to act as a manure-strewn escape route for riders drifting too wide. 🚫 👁 Popular with photographers, comply with warning signs.

Ballabeg Hairpin
A snaking, bumpy approach brings riders suddenly upon this sharp turn to the right, where the circuit joins the A7 in Ballabeg village. Viewing from behind walls and barriers on the outside.
🍴 ☕ P 👁 Slow corner, difficult to get shots other than bikes from behind.

Ballawhetstone-William's Corner – Billown Dip
Some spectating possible along this stretch, no access when roads closed. Take note of prohibited area signs.
🚫 👁 The awesome Billown Dip is shaded by trees (riders call it the Black Hole), so too dark in the evening.

Cross Four Ways
Third of the four major right-handers, turning onto the A3 road towards Castletown. Clear views from behind barriers on the outside of the circuit. Accessible from the A3 and only ¾ mile (1km) from Ballasalla village on the A7. There is parking on these roads, but allow for a walk down to the corner.
🍴 ☕ P 👁 Hard braking on the approach can be dramatic, but more scope at Church Bends.

Church Bends
Cresting a ridge brings riders to this severe right and left esses past Malew Church, with spectating possible from behind walls in fields and the church grounds. Limited parking nearby, or walk from Cross Four Ways. Respect church and farm property.

🚫 👁 Probably the best place for photos, with several angles possible.

Great Meadow
A gentle sweep to the right under trees. This point and Church Bends can be reached by a footpath from Ronaldsway Airport: arrive before the roads close to find a spot where spectating is permitted. 🚫

Stadium Bend
Machines can be seen approaching down a straight before banking through the left-hander perilously close to stone walls at the apex. Good views from behind walls on both sides.
🍴 P 👁 Great shots possible, but it's scary here.

Castletown Corner
At the last sharp right on the circuit, it bridges the steam railway track before rejoining the A5. Popular vantage point with viewing on the outside of the corner, from a paid-for seat on the 200-seat stand located on a grass area directly overlooking the exit, from the end of Malew Street or from a small area behind the bridge parapet. Parking places can be found in the area and the centre of Castletown is only a few minutes' walk away.
🍴 ☕ P WC 👁 Good for capturing riders making a last desperate effort before taking the chequered flag.

BILLOWN CIRCUIT		
The ten fastest riders		
1 Guy Martin	114.245mph	2013
2 Michael Dunlop	113.922mph	2013
3 Dean Harrison	113.461mph	2013
4 Conor Cummins	112.257mph	2012
5 Ryan Farquhar	112.199mph	2011
6 William Dunlop	112.136mph	2011
7 Ian Lougher	111.883mph	2005
8 Cameron Donald	111.265mph	2006
9 Jamie Hamilton	110.512mph	2013
10 Jason Griffiths	110.279mph	2005

Die Billown Circuit

In Billown ist die Auswahl an Aussichtspunkten kleiner als bei der Bergstrecke, es ist jedoch sehr spannend, die Fahrer auf der schwierigen Strecke zu beobachten, insbesondere da das Feld gemeinsam startet. Die Straßen werden nicht wie an der größeren Strecke tageweise gesperrt, deshalb läuft man nicht Gefahr, an einem unzugänglichen Ort ohne Erfrischungen und Toiletten festzusitzen. Das Geld, das für die beiden großen Tribünen am Start und an Castletown Corner berechnet wird, dient der Begleichung der Mietkosten und Organisation zukünftiger Treffen. Der Southern 100 Club besitzt und betreibt Imbissstände am Start/Ziel, in Ballabeg und an der Kreuzung Cross Four Ways.

Das Manx Radio berichtet über die Rennen und es gibt Lautsprecheranlagen am Start/Ziel. Mit einer Live-Timing-App für die meisten modernen Smartphones werden Sie Runde um Runde über alle Rennen auf dem Laufenden gehalten. Sie können die App gegen eine kleine Gebühr unter www.mylaps.com herunterladen.

Start und Ziel
An der Start-/Ziellinie, welche sich auf einer von Castletown Corner bergab führenden Geraden befindet, gibt es eine große Tribüne mit 200 Sitzplätzen. Hinter den Absperrungen gibt es Stehplätze auf der Wiese zwischen Tribüne und Rennzentrale mit Fahrerlager, wo die Arbory Road auf die Castletown-Zufahrt der A5 führt.

Hier haben Sie eine tolle Sicht auf hektische Starts und aufregende Zieleinfahrten, die typisch für Billown-Rennen sind. Außerdem sind Sie nahe am Fahrerlager, so dass Sie die Maschinen aus der Nähe sehen können.

🏍 🏁 P wc 👁 Die Abendsonne verleiht Bildern der Massenstarts eine besondere Atmosphäre.

Ballakeighan
Nach der Start-/Zielgeraden folgt auf die Rechtskurve an der Ballakeighan Farm eine schnelle, leicht ansteigende Linksbiegung. Hier kann es während der ersten Runde brenzlig werden, werden die Fahrer der Spitzengruppe hier auf die Ideallinie drängen. Man kann hier und an der Zufahrt hinter Mauern zuschauen.

🏍 P 👁 Während der ersten Runde lassen sich hier gut dicht beieinander fahrende Gruppen fotografieren.

Iron Gates
Eine 750 m lange Gerade verläuft leicht bergab zu dem gefährlichen Rechtsknick mit einer Steinmauer und ohne inneren Seitenstreifen.

🚫 👁 Besonders aufregende Bilder erhalten Sie, wenn Sie festhalten können, wie die Motorräder in der Kurve innen an der Mauer entlang schrammen. Auch ein weiter Blick die Gerade hinauf ist möglich.

Conor Cummins, Ballakeighan, Southern 100

Ballanorris
Eine baumbeschattete Linksbiegung führt an dem Bauernhof vorbei. Ein offenes Tor führt zu einem Feld am Ausgang, das Fahrern, die zu weit abdriften, als dungbestreute Ausweichmöglichkeit dient. ⊘ ◉ Bei Fotografen beliebt, halten Sie sich an die Warnschilder.

Ballabeg Hairpin
Über eine gewundene, wellige Zufahrt nähren sich die Fahrer dieser plötzlichen, steilen Rechtskurve, an der die Strecke im Dorf Ballabeg auf die A7 stößt. Man kann außerhalb der Strecke hinter Mauern und Absperrungen zuschauen. ⊷ ⯑ P ◉ Langsame Kurve, die Motorräder können nur von hinten fotografiert werden.

Ballawhetstone-William's Corner – Billown Dip
Auf diesem Abschnitt ist das Zuschauen eingeschränkt möglich. Kein Zugang wenn die Straßen gesperrt sind. Auf Schilder für gesperrte Gebiete achten.
⊘ ◉ Die respekteinflößende Senke Billown Dip wird von Bäumen überschattet (die Fahrer nennen sie „schwarzes Loch"), deshalb ist es abends zum Fotografieren zu dunkel.

Cross Four Ways
In der dritten von vier großen Rechtskurven wendet sich die Strecke auf die A3 nach Castletown. Freie Sicht hinter Absperrungen außerhalb der Strecke. Zugänglich von der A3 und nur ca. 1 km vom Dorf Ballasalla an der A7 entfernt. Es gibt Parkmöglichkeiten an den Straßen, man muss aber mit einem Fußweg zur Kurve rechnen.
⊷ ⯑ P ◉ Auf der Zufahrt heftig abbremsende Motorräder können effektvoll aussehen, aber an Church Bends gibt es abwechslungsreichere Motive.

Church Bends
Nachdem die Fahrer einen Hügel überqueren, gelangen sie an diese steile Rechtskurve und nach links weisenden S-Kurven hinter der Kirche von Malew. Zuschauer können sich hinter Mauern auf Feldern und dem Kirchengelände aufhalten. Beschränkte Parkmöglichkeiten in der Nähe oder zu Fuß vom Cross Four Ways erreichbar.
Halten Sie sich an die Regeln hinsichtlich des Kirchen- und Agrargeländes.

⊘ ◉ Die wahrscheinlich beste Stelle zum Fotografieren, unterschiedliche Blickwinkel möglich.

Great Meadow
Eine sanfte Rechtskurve unter Bäumen. Dieser Bereich und Church Bends sind über einen Fußweg vom Flughafen Ronaldsway erreichbar, Sie müssen jedoch vor Sperrung der Straßen eintreffen und sich eine Stelle suchen, an dem das Zuschauen gestattet ist. ⊘

Stadium Bend
Man sieht die Maschinen über eine Gerade näher kommen, ehe sie durch die Linkskurve fahren, wobei sie am Scheitelpunkt gefährlich nahe an die Mauern kommen. Hinter Mauern auf beiden Straßenseiten ist die Sicht gut. ⊷ P ◉ Hier sind gute Bilder möglich, es ist hier aber furchteinflößend.

Castletown Corner
An der letzten steilen Rechtskurve führt die Strecke über die Dampfeisenbahnstrecke und führt dann auf die A5. Zuschauen kann man von einem beliebten Aussichtspunkt außerhalb der Kurve, einer kostenpflichtigen Tribüne mit 200 Sitzplätzen auf einer Wiese direkt am Ausgang, vom Ende der Malew Street oder von einem kleinen Bereich hinter dem Brückengeländer. Es gibt in der Gegend Parkplätze und die Innenstadt von Castletown ist nur einige Gehminuten entfernt.
⊷ ⯑ P WC ◉ Hier kann man gut fotografieren, wie sich die Fahrer noch ein letztes Mal ins Zeug legen, ehe sie ins Ziel fahren.

BILLOWN CIRCUIT Die zehn schnellsten Fahrer			
1	Guy Martin	114.245mph	2013
2	Michael Dunlop	113.922mph	2013
3	Dean Harrison	113.461mph	2013
4	Conor Cummins	112.257mph	2012
5	Ryan Farquhar	112.199mph	2011
6	William Dunlop	112.136mph	2011
7	Ian Lougher	111.883mph	2005
8	Cameron Donald	111.265mph	2006
9	Jamie Hamilton	110.512mph	2013
10	Jason Griffiths	110.279mph	2005

■ ▪

Le Billown Circuit

Billown a moins de points de vue que la Mountain Course mais regarder les pilotes sur le circuit exigeant est toujours excitant, notamment lorsque les concurrents démarrent en peloton. La fermeture des routes durant le plus grand circuit ne dure pas toute la journée. Si vous restez bloqués à un endroit inaccessible sans collation ou commodités ce n'est pas un problème. Le montant facturé pour les deux tribunes au départ et au Castletown Corner sert à organiser de prochaines rencontres après que les frais de location ont été couverts. Le Southern 100 Club possède et exploite des établissements gastronomiques au départ/à l'arrivée, Ballabeg et Cross Four Ways.

La Manx Rado couvre le racing et un système de sonorisation se trouve au départ/à l'arrivée. Une application compatible avec la majorité des smart phones les plus récent vous permet de suivre la course en direct. Téléchargement sur www.mylaps.com pour une somme modique.

Départ et arrivée
Une tribune pouvant recevoir environ 200 personnes donne sur la ligne de départ/d'arrivée, située sur une ligne droite avec une descente à partir du Castletown

Corner. Un espace avec des places debout se trouve derrière les barrières sur la zone gazonnée située entre la tribune et le PC course et la zone de paddock, située là où la Arbory Road rejoint la route de contournement A5 de Castletown.

Une vue magnifique des départs effrénés et des arrivées excitantes, une caractéristique du racing de Billown, et à proximité du paddock vous pourrez voire les machines de près. ➔ ⚡ P wc 👁 Le soleil couchant renforce l'effet des lieux de démarrage en peloton.

Ballakeighan
La courbe à droite à hauteur de la ferme de Ballakeighan suit une courbe à gauche légèrement montante suivant la ligne droite de départ et d'arrivée. Il peut s'avérer que l'on ressente un vrai frissonnement au premier tour lorsque le groupe de tête arrive dans la lutte pour passer au mieux la ligne. Vues de derrière les murs ici et sur l'approche.
➔ P 👁 Exceptionnel pour les prises de vue de groupes qui ne semblent pas vraiment se départager au premier tour.

Porte en fer
Une ligne droite d'un demi-mile (750 m) descend doucement vers la terrifiante boucle à droite avec un

Ryan Farquhar, Billown Dip, Southern 100

mur en pierre et aucune bordure de trottoir à l'intérieur.

⊘ 👁 Pour le fun, surprenez les motos rasant l'intérieur du mur dans le virage. Ou prenez des vues longue portée en regardant la ligne droite.

Ballanorris

Une courbe à gauche après le passage de la ferme à l'ombre des arbres. Un accès à un terrain à la sortie reste ouvert pour servir de voie d'évacuation parsemé d'engrais pour les pilotes faisant un trop gros écart. ⊘ 👁 Populaire auprès des photographes, respectez les panneaux d'avertissement.

Ballabeg Hairpin

Une approche cahoteuse sinueuse déporte les pilotes subitement vers la droite dans le virage serré où le circuit joint l'A7 dans le Ballabeg village. Vue par derrière les murs et barrières à l'extérieur. Vues de derrière les murs ici et sur l'approche.

🏍 ♨ P 👁 Virage lent, emplacements difficiles d'accès par l'arrière autre qu'avec des motos.

Ballawhetstone-William's Corner – Billown Dip

Plusieurs emplacements pour regarder le long de cette section, aucun accès lorsque les routes sont fermées. Respectez les panneaux des zones interdites.

⊘ 👁 L'impressionnant Billown Dip se trouve à l'ombre des arbres (les pilotes le nomment Black Hole), tellement il est sombre en fin de soirée.

Cross Four Ways

Trois des quatre grands virages à droite tournent vers la route A3 menant vers Castletown. Vues dégagées par derrière les barrières à l'extérieur du circuit. Accessible de l'A3 et à seulement 3/4 mile (1 km) du Ballasalla village sur l'A7. Stationnement possible sur ces routes mais prévoyez de descendre à pied au virage. 🏍 ♨ P 👁 Un freinage brusque à l'approche peut être dramatique, mais plus d'espace à Church Bends.

Church Bends

Une crête mène les pilotes à ces esses difficiles à gauche et à droite après le passage de la Malew Church, possibilité d'apprécier la course par derrière les murs dans les champs et sur les terrains de l'église. Stationnement limité à proximité, ou partez de Cross

Four Ways. Respectez la propriété de l'église et de la ferme. ⊘ 👁 Probablement le meilleur endroit pour prendre des photos avec plusieurs angles possibles.

Great Meadow

Une courbe douce vers la droite sous les arbres. Cet endroit et Church Bends sont accessibles par une passerelle de l'aéroport de Ronaldsway : arrivez avant que les routes soient fermées pour trouver un endroit autorisé aux spectateurs. ⊘

Stadium Bend

Il est possible de voir l'approche des machines dangereusement proches des murs de pierre au sommet en descendant la ligne droite avant de virer par la gauche. Bonnes vues des deux côtés par derrière les murs.

🏍 P 👁 Possibilité de prendre des photos magnifiques mais c'est effrayant ici.

Castletown Corner

Au dernier tournant serré à droite du circuit, il chevauche la voie de chemin de fer à vapeur avant de rejoindre l'A5. Point de vue apprécié avec une vision sur l'extérieur du virage d'une tribune de 200 places située sur la zone gazonnée donnant directement sur la sortie au bout de la Malew Street, ou d'une petite zone située derrière le parapet du pont. Il est possible de trouver des places de stationnement dans la zone, et le centre de Castletown est à quelques minutes à pied. 🏍 ♨ P WC 👁 Convient pour capturer les pilotes faisant une dernière tentative désespérée avant de saisir le drapeau à damiers.

BILLOWN CIRCUIT Les dix pilotes plus rapides			
1	Guy Martin	114.245mph	2013
2	Michael Dunlop	113.922mph	2013
3	Dean Harrison	113.461mph	2013
4	Conor Cummins	112.257mph	2012
5	Ryan Farquhar	112.199mph	2011
6	William Dunlop	112.136mph	2011
7	Ian Lougher	111.883mph	2005
8	Cameron Donald	111.265mph	2006
9	Jamie Hamilton	110.512mph	2013
10	Jason Griffiths	110.279mph	2005

Circuito de Billown

Billown ofrece una menor selección de puntos para seguir las carreras que el circuito de la montaña; no obstante, siempre resulta emocionante ver actuar a los pilotos en este circuito tan exigente, especialmente con parrillas de salida. No se realizan cierres de carreteras que duran todo el día como sucede con el circuito de la montaña, por lo que no existe problema de quedarse aislado en un punto inaccesible sin posibilidad de tomarse un refrigerio o ir al aseo. Existen dos tribunas de pago, una en la salida y otra en Castletown Corner; la recaudación va destinada a la organización de futuras carreras una vez cubiertos los gastos de alquiler. El Southern 100 Club es el propietario y explotador de los establecimientos de comida sitos en la salida/meta, en Ballabeg y en Cross Four Ways.

Manx Radio ofrece cobertura de las carreras y hay megafonía en la salida/meta. Existe una aplicación compatible con la mayoría de smartphones actuales que le permitirá conocer en directo los tiempos vuelta a vuelta y estar al tanto de cada carrera. Puede descargarla en www.mylaps.com por un módico precio.

Salida y meta
La línea de salida/meta cuenta con una tribuna para 200 personas sentadas; está situada en la recta que se inicia con el descenso desde Castletown Corner. Hay un sitio para seguir las carreras detrás de las barreras protectoras en la zona de hierba entre la tribuna y la zona del cuartel general de carrera y del paddock, ubicado en la unión de Arbory Road con la circunvalación A5 de Castletown.

Grandes vistas de las frenéticas salidas y las emocionantes llegadas, uno de los puntos fuertes de las carreras de Billown; proximidad al paddock para contemplar de cerca las motos. 🏍 ♨ P WC 👁 El sol vespertino añade emoción a las imágenes de las parrillas de salida.

Ballakeighan
La curva de derechas de la granja de Ballakeighan sigue a un rápido giro de izquierdas ligeramente en subida tras la recta de salida y meta. Este punto pone los pelos de punta en la primera vuelta cuando se ve aparecer al grupo de cabeza peleando en busca de la mejor trazada. Vistas desde detrás de los muros y en la aproximación. 🏍 P 👁 Excelente punto para realizar fotos de grupos muy compactos en la primera vuelta.

Puertas de hierro
Recta de media milla (750 m) ligeramente en bajada que va a dar a una espeluznante curva de derechas

Jamie Hamilton, Church Bends, Southern 100

junto a un muro de piedra; no hay bordillo en el interior. ⊘ ☞ Para reflejar toda la espectacularidad, intente captar cómo rozan las motos desde dentro del muro en la curva. También puede tomar vistas amplias de la recta previa.

Ballanorris
Un giro de izquierdas entre árboles pasada la granja. El portón de un prado en la salida de la curva permanece abierto a modo de escapatoria para los pilotos que hacen un recto. ⊘ ☞ Popular entre los fotógrafos; respete las señales de aviso.

Ballabeg Hairpin
Una aproximación sinuosa y bacheada lleva bruscamente a los pilotos a esta cerrada curva de derechas donde el circuito se junta con la A7 en la localidad de Ballabeg. Buena visión detrás de muros y barreras en el exterior. 🏍 ⚡ P ☞ Curva lenta, complicado realizar fotos que no sean desde detrás de las motos.

Ballawhetstone-William's Corner – Billown Dip
Es posible seguir las carreras en este tramo; sin acceso cuando se cierran las carreteras. Tenga presente las señales indicadoras de área prohibida. ⊘ ☞ El increíble Billown Dip transcurre entre árboles (los pilotos lo denominan el "agujero negro"), de modo que la visibilidad es mínima cuando oscurece.

Cross Four Ways
La tercera de las cuatro principales curvas de derechas; al girar se sale a la A3 en dirección a Castletown. Buenas vistas desde detrás de las barreras en el exterior del circuito. Acceso desde la A3; a solo 3/4 de milla (1 km) de Ballasalla por la A7. Estas carreteras disponen de aparcamiento, pero debe caminarse para llegar a la curva. 🏍 ⚡ P ☞ La fuerte frenada de aproximación resulta espectacular; no obstante, Church Bends ofrece más posibilidades.

Church Bends
Una rasante lleva a los pilotos a este tramo de complicadas "eses" de derechas e izquierdas pasando por Malew Church; es posible seguir la competición detrás de los muros de los campos y de los jardines de la iglesia. Poco aparcamiento en las proximidades; también puede caminarse desde Cross Four Ways.

Respete los campos y los terrenos de la iglesia. ⊘ ☞ Probablemente el mejor lugar para hacer fotos; varios ángulos posibles.

Great Meadow
Una suave curva de derechas bajo los árboles. El acceso a este punto y a Church Bends se realiza a través de un sendero desde el aeropuerto de Ronaldsway; llegue antes de que se cierren las carreteras para encontrar un sitio donde esté permitido seguir la competición. ⊘

Stadium Bend
Puede verse cómo se aproximan las motos por la recta antes de trazar esta peligrosa curva de izquierdas cuyo ápice está muy próximo a los muros de piedra. Buenas vistas tras los muros en ambos lados. 🏍 P ☞ Pueden obtenerse excelentes fotos, pero el sitio asusta.

Castletown Corner
Última curva cerrada de derechas del circuito; salva la vía del ferrocarril de vapor antes de volver a la A5. Una posición muy popular con vistas en el exterior de la curva desde una tribuna de pago con 200 asientos en una zona de hierba que da directamente a la salida, desde el final de Malew Street o desde un pequeño punto detrás del parapeto del puente. Hay plazas de aparcamiento en la zona y el centro de Castletown se encuentra a solo unos minutos caminando. 🏍 ⚡ P WC ☞ Buen sitio para captar a los pilotos en un último y desesperado intento antes de la bandera de cuadros.

BILLOWN CIRCUIT
Los diez pilotos más rápidos

1	Guy Martin	114.245mph	2013
2	Michael Dunlop	113.922mph	2013
3	Dean Harrison	113.461mph	2013
4	Conor Cummins	112.257mph	2012
5	Ryan Farquhar	112.199mph	2011
6	William Dunlop	112.136mph	2011
7	Ian Lougher	111.883mph	2005
8	Cameron Donald	111.265mph	2006
9	Jamie Hamilton	110.512mph	2013
10	Jason Griffiths	110.279mph	2005

What to do when there are no races?

ANCIENT SITES & MONUMENTS

Freely-accessible sites include Balladoole (dating from prehistoric to Viking times) near Castletown, Cronk ny Merriu (Iron Age fort) at Port Grenaugh between Douglas and Derbyhaven, The Braaid (Iron Age and Norse settlement) west of Douglas, St Michael's Isle (12th-century chapel and 16th-century fort) at Langness, Mull Hill (Neolithic burial chambers) near Cregneash, King Orry's Grave at Laxey, 14th-century Monks Bridge at Ballasalla and the Neolithic chambered tomb of Cashtal yn Ard near Glen Mona.

The Island has over 200 ancient decorated stone crosses. Most remain in churches and churchyard cross shelters of their parish of origin.

THE GREAT LAXEY WHEEL

Also known as Lady Isabella, the world's largest working waterwheel. 72 feet in diameter with 95 steps leading to a viewing platform 75 feet above the ground with breathtaking views.

CAMERA OBSCURA

Reopened in 2005 after major restoration, the Great Union Camera Obscura on Douglas Head was built for the Victorian tourism boom. It gives spectacular views over Douglas. Open May to September, Saturdays 1pm-4pm; Sundays and bank holidays 11am-4pm.

CASTLES

Castle Rushen, which gave its name to Castletown, is one of Europe's best-preserved 12th century fortresses. The oldest part of the castle is believed to have been built during the time of Magnus, last Viking King of Mann. The castle was developed by successive rulers for 300 years, being surrendered to parliamentary

forces during the English Civil War. The castle has also served as a centre of administration, a mint, a law court and a prison. Today it is a major visitor attraction, showing life as it was for the kings and Lords of Mann.

Peel Castle stands on St Patrick's Isle, which was a centre of Manx Christianity in the 6th century. Major excavation in the 1980s revealed Viking jewellery and other finds, now on display in the Manx Museum, Douglas. The story of St Patrick's Isle is introduced in Peel's House of Manannan.

MANX ELECTRIC RAILWAY

The 1893 Manx Electric Railway runs for almost 18 miles between Douglas and Ramsey, with magnificent views along the east coast. At Laxey you can transfer to the Snaefell Mountain Railway. With the two oldest working tramcars in the world, it is the longest vintage narrow-gauge line in the British Isles.

GROUDLE RAILWAY

Lovingly restored by volunteers, the 2 feet gauge line north of Douglas climbs out of the glen's lower reaches and winds along the edge of the hillside to the cliff-top terminus where you can enjoy the fantastic views.

SNAEFELL MOUNTAIN RAILWAY

The electric 1895 Snaefell Mountain Railway is unique in the British Isles. The ascent up the side of Laxey Glen is slow and gradual over almost 5 miles, with views of Laxey Wheel. The line crosses the TT course at the Bungalow station before climbing to more than 2,000 feet above sea level at the Summit Café. On a clear day you can see the Island below you and beyond, England, Scotland, Ireland and Wales.

STEAM RAILWAY

Opened in 1874, the Isle of Man Steam Railway is the oldest surviving Manx railway. The railway has been granted a new lease of life with the largest reinvestment in renewal and maintenance since it was built.

The station at Port Erin has a café and a museum of railway memorabilia. Douglas terminus also has a café.

FARM & ANIMAL ATTRACTIONS
Curraghs Wildlife Park

More than 100 species of birds and animals from wetland areas around the world, along with nature and butterfly trails and the Island's smallest passenger-carrying railway. Open all year, Easter to October 10am-6pm; winter weekends only 10am-4pm.
www.gov.im/categories/leisure-and-entertainment/curraghs-wildlife-park/

The Mann Cat Sanctuary

Located in Santon, between Douglas and Castletown. www.manncat.com

The Home of Rest for Old Horses

Located on Richmond Hill just outside Douglas. The retirement destination for the tram-pulling shires. Café, facilities for the disabled and plenty of car parking.
www.iom-horseshome.com

WILDLIFE & NATURE RESERVES

Basking sharks, seals, hen harriers, choughs, gannets, mountain hares, mountain goats, wallabies – on the Isle of Man you can see them all.

Basking sharks attracted to the waters of the south and west coasts are regular visitors about mid-summer. They feed just below the surface on microscopic plants and animals and are easy to spot. You may also spy seals at the Sound in the south and the Ayres in the north.

Manx Wildlife Trust has 20 nature reserves, including Close Sartfield – the largest winter hen harrier roost in western Europe. Details of these reserves are available at the Trust Shop, 7-8 Market Street, Peel.

The Calf of Man, a 600 acre nature reserve and bird sanctuary, has been an official British Bird Observatory since 1962. Rare native Manx Loaghtan sheep are kept here, distinctive for their rams, which have four or even six horns.

GLENS

Seventeen designated national glens are owned and protected by the Manx government and preserved in their natural state. These havens of peace and tranquillity are some of the Island's most visited attractions, several glens being famous for their spectacular waterfalls.

MUSEUMS
A.R.E. Motorcycle Collection – Kirk Michael

Private collection of over 100 vintage motorcycles at Kirk Michael. Open Sunday afternoons 2pm-5pm from Easter to September. www.aremuseum.com

Grove Museum of Victorian Life – Ramsey.
Victorian time capsule of fine period furnishings in an elegant country house set in lovely gardens. http://www.manxnationalheritage.im/attractions/grove-museum-of-victorian-life/

House of Manannan – Peel.
See Manannan and hear his own gripping story of how the early Manx Celts and Viking settlers shaped the Island's history. This interactive heritage centre uses audio, video and state-of-the-art display techniques to inform and entertain. http://www.manxnationalheritage.im/attractions/house-of-manannan/

Jurby Transport Museum – Jurby.
Created by the Manx Transport Trust at Jurby Airfield and dedicated to the Island's road transport heritage, particularly buses. The Trust aims to salvage, preserve and display as many vehicles as possible. Summer opening times: Tuesday, Saturday, Sunday and Bank Holidays 10am-4pm. www.jtmiom.im

Isle of Man Motor Museum
The Isle of Man Motor Museum is the latest attraction to be housed in Jurby, and is the home of the Cunningham Classic Car Collection. Comprised of over 100 vehicles, what began as a small collection of classic cars, started 30 years ago by Denis Cunningham, is now the passion of both Denis and his son Darren. Concentrating on rare and unique models from all over the world. Over 250 vehicles are on display, from classic cars and racing motorcycles to larger items such as a Greyhound Bus, fire engines and a steam collection. Set in an exhibition space of over 70,000 sq. ft the ground floor displays a large number of vehicles, with motorcycles being housed on a mezzanine floor. Facilities include a gift shop, refreshment area, toilets, and a car club display area. Admission prices and further information are available from the website http://www.isleofmanmotormuseum.com or https://www.facebook.com/isleofmanmotormuseum

Kipper Factory & Museum – Peel.
Working demonstration of how herring are prepared and oak-smoked to produce delicious Manx kippers. www.manxkippers.com

Leece Museum – Peel.
The story of Peel as revealed in a unique collection of old photographs. www.peelonline.net/leece/

Manx Aviation Museum and the Museum of the Manx Regiment – Ballasalla.
Records Manx wartime and civil aviation history. The Museum of the Manx Regiment delves into the Isle of Man's military history. www.iomguide.com/aviationmilitarymuseum.php

Manx Museum & Art Gallery – Douglas.
Presents 10,000 years of the Island's history through a vast collection of artefacts. www.manxnationalheritage.im/attractions/ manx-museum/

Manx Transport Museum – Peel.
Small museum, representing all forms of Manx transport, including a P50 – the world's smallest road-legal car, made in Peel in 1964. Features historical movie clips, photos and collectibles. http://www.visitisleofman.com/placestovisit/museums/manxtransport.xml

National Folk Museum – Cregneash.
Authentic village of thatched whitewashed cottages, a popular film location, uses traditional farming methods to show how 19th-century Manx crofters lived and worked. Britain's first open-air museum. http://www.manxnationalheritage.im/ attractions/cregneash/

Nautical Museum – Castletown.
Dedicated to the amazing story of *Peggy* – an historic 18th-century vessel involved in local smuggling but walled up in her boathouse and undiscovered for a hundred years. http://www.manxnationalheritage.im/ attractions/nautical-museum/

The Old Grammar School – Castletown.
Built as a chapel in about 1200, this small whitewashed building changed its role many times over the centuries. It was used as a school from 1570. http://www.manxnationalheritage.im/attractions/old-grammar-school/

The Old House of Keys – Castletown.
This restored 1820 building was once the assembly and debating chamber for part of the Manx Parliament. A Manx National Heritage attraction. http://www.manxnationalheritage.im/attractions/old-house-of-keys/

PARKS & GARDENS
Children love parks for the opportunity to let off steam while adults are often content to simply relax and appreciate the peace, quiet and colour of gardens created by experts.

For fun and activities:
Noble's Park, Douglas – behind the Grandstand in Douglas. Tennis and netball courts, bowling green, skate park, BMX track and two modern children's playgrounds. Restaurant and café.

Onchan Park, Onchan. Boating lake complete with bumper and motorboats. Go-karts, crazy golf and large children's playground. Onchan Raceway is also here – the home of stockcar racing, Formula 2s, Ministox, Hot Rods and banger racing.

Silverdale Glen, near Ballasalla. Boating lake, historical glen, picnic areas and a children's play area. Also includes popular Craftworks, where youngsters can create their own piece based on local Manx designs.

Mooragh Park, Ramsey. 12-acre boating lake ideal for beginners in canoeing and sailing. 40 acres of parkland. Bowling, crazy golf, tennis courts, BMX course and skate park. Large children's playground and water play area. Restaurant and café.

For horticultural gardens, it's hard to beat those at Laxey, laid out on the old washing floors of the mines, or the beautiful setting of historic St John's. The village's Tynwald National Park & Arboretum contains many species of exotic trees. At Tynwald Mills Centre you can enjoy the Manx Wild Flower Garden.

The sunken gardens at Douglas are a riot of colour in spring and summer and are often designed and planted to reflect the theme of notable anniversaries and occasions.

SHOPPING
Douglas has two shopping centres – the Strand and the Tower House galleria plus three supermarkets.

Laxey is well known for genuine Manx tweeds produced at St George's Woollen Mills. But perhaps the biggest shopping surprise of all is to be found at the Tynwald Mills Centre – an attractive selection of shops sharing the old mill buildings in St John's, a few miles inland from Peel. Food, fashion, furniture, houseware, gifts, garden products and pet products are all on sale in a cosy and relaxed environment.

VISITOR CENTRES
Scarlett Visitor Centre near Castletown explains how volcanic activity created spectacular local rock formations about 250 million years ago.

The Sound Visitor Centre and Restaurant near Cregneash features a panoramic window looking out across the tidal waters of the Sound to the Calf of Man.

Niarbyl has a visitor centre and café. Situated on an important geological site, this is the perfect spot for watching marine wildlife.

The Ayres Visitor Centre, run by Manx Wildlife Trust, explains the significance of the Ayres National Nature Reserve and its unique variety of habitats and sensitive ecosystem.

Visitor Safety for
Open and Closed Roads

The Isle of Man Constabulary wishes all visitors to the Island a safe and enjoyable time whilst at the TT Festival.

One of the unique features of the TT Festival is that the circuit of 37.73 miles is run entirely on public roads, to which the general public have access whilst the roads are open. We must stress that at these times the roads are completely subject to Road Traffic law, which is rigidly enforced to keep people safe.

The majority of Manx Road Traffic Legislation is identical to that in the United Kingdom, and ignorance is not a defence.

To this end, please:

On open roads:
- Adhere to all speed limits and signage.
- Ride to the conditions.
- Ride or drive within your own ability. This is especially important when riding with friends or in a group.
- Please remember these are public roads and they are used by all members of the general public including farmers etc. Be aware there could be farm vehicles or other slow moving vehicles round the corner. Expect the unexpected!
- With the higher volume of traffic using the roads, be prepared for queues at roundabouts and junctions.
- On right-hand bends made sure that both yourself and your machine, and not just your tyres, are completely on your own side of the centre lines.
- The TT Festival attracts visitors from far and wide, many of whom may not be used to riding on the left-hand side of the road. With this in mind, please take extra care when approaching areas where journeys might start, for example campsites.

Any driving ban imposed by an Isle of Man Court is applicable in the UK as there is now a reciprocal agreement in place so a moment of madness on the Island's roads could cost you dearly in the long term.

At the races:
- The TT Races is one of the greatest spectator sports in the world. Nowhere do you get as close to the action as you would sitting on a hedge on the Isle of Man surrounded by breath-taking scenery as the world's leading motorcycle road racers past you.

- However, TT race spectators have a responsibility to themselves, the marshals and the riders to watch the races in a responsible manner. Motorsport is dangerous and while the organisers recognise that you want to get as close to the action as possible you must follow the rules. If in doubt speak to the marshals in the area; they are there for the safety of the riders and the spectators.

- Choose your position carefully and consider your safety. The position that gives a great view may not be the safest position to view from. A motorcycle travelling at 100mph is covering over 44 metres every second and on the faster sections of the course the motorcycles can reach speeds in the region of 200mph. If, unfortunately something did go wrong, ask yourself – "Would I have time to react and move?" If the answer is no then you are probably in an unsafe position.

- In the interests of spectator safety, you will see that the organisers have marked certain areas around the course with "Restricted Area" or "Prohibited Area" markers. As a result areas that you may have previously watched from may now be prohibited. You must respect the marshal's advice and look for an alternative viewing area. With a track stretching to over 37 miles you are not short of choices!

- Once the roads are closed do not go onto them. Walking or encroaching onto a closed road could result in you being prosecuted and facing a heavy fine up to £2,500.

Finally, whilst soaking up the atmosphere of the TT Festival you may fancy a beer or two. If you are going to drink alcohol please don't ride afterwards. Allow sufficient time for the alcohol to get out of your system. The penalties for riding over the prescribed limit on the Isle of Man are similar to those in the UK with, at minimum, a twelve month driving ban.

Sicherheit von Besuchern auf offenen und gesperrten Straßen

Die Polizei der Isle of Man wünscht allen Besuchern des TT-Festivals einen sicheren und angenehmen Aufenthalt.

Eine Besonderheit des TT-Festivals ist die Tatsache, dass die 60,7 km lange Strecke vollständig auf öffentlichen Straßen verläuft, zu denen jeder Zugang hat, wenn sie offen sind. Wir möchten deshalb besonders darauf hinweisen, dass die Straßen vollständig dem Straßenverkehrsrecht unterliegen, das aus Sicherheitsgründen streng durchgesetzt wird.

Das Straßenverkehrsrecht auf der Isle of Man entspricht weitgehend den im Vereinigten Königreich geltenden Gesetzen. Unkenntnis schützt nicht vor Strafe.

Deshalb beachten Sie bitte folgende Vorschriften:
Auf offenen Straßen:
- Beachten Sie alle Geschwindigkeitsbegrenzungen und Verkehrsschilder.
- Fahren Sie den Straßenverhältnissen entsprechend.
- Fahren Sie entsprechend Ihrer Fähigkeiten. Dies ist besonders wichtig, wenn Sie mit Freunden oder in der Gruppe mit dem Motorrad unterwegs sind.
- Beachten Sie, dass es sich um öffentliche Straßen handelt, die allen Verkehrsteilnehmern, einschließlich Landwirten usw. zugänglich sind. Seien Sie darauf vorbereitet, dass sich hinter einer Kurve Landwirtschaftsfahrzeuge oder andere langsame Fahrzeuge befinden können. Erwarten Sie das Unerwartete!
- Rechnen Sie bei erhöhtem Verkehrsaufkommen mit Staus an Verkehrskreiseln und Kreuzungen.
- Achten Sie bei Rechtskurven darauf, dass sowohl Sie als auch Ihr Fahrzeug und nicht nur die Räder sich vollständig auf Ihrer Seite der Mittellinie befinden.
- Das TT-Festival zieht internationale Besucher an, von denen viele nicht an Linksverkehr gewöhnt sind. Beachten Sie dies und seien Sie bitte an Stellen, wo sich möglicherweise Besucher dem Verkehr anschließen, wie an Campingplätzen, besonders vorsichtig.

Fahrverbote, die von einem Gericht der Isle of Man verhängt werden, gelten auch in Großbritannien, da es hierzu eine gegenseitige Abmachung gibt. Deshalb kann Sie ein Moment der Unachtsamkeit auf der Insel auch auf lange Sicht teuer zu stehen kommen.

Bei den Rennen:
- Die TT-Rennen gehören zu den beliebtesten Zuschauersportarten der Welt. Nirgends sind Sie so nah am Geschehen wie auf der Isle of Man, wenn Sie auf der Böschung inmitten der atemberaubenden Landschaft sitzen und die besten Straßenrennfahrer der Welt an Ihnen vorbei sausen.
- Besucher der TT-Rennen sind jedoch sich selbst, den Ordnern und den Fahren gegenüber dafür verantwortlich, die Rennen auf verantwortungsvolle Weise zu schauen. Der Motorsport ist gefährlich und obwohl die Veranstalter wissen, dass Sie so nahe wie möglich an der Action sein wollen, müssen Sie die Regeln befolgen. Wenden Sie sich bei Fragen an einen Ordner in der Nähe, sie sind für die Sicherheit der Fahrer und Zuschauer zuständig.
- Wählen Sie sorgfältig eine Stelle zum Zusehen aus und berücksichtigen Sie dabei Ihre Sicherheit. Eine Stelle mit guter Sicht, ist nicht unbedingt sicher. Ein Motorrad, das mit ca. 160 km/h fährt, legt 44 Meter pro Sekunde zurück. Auf den schnellen Streckenabschnitten erreichen die Motorräder sogar Geschwindigkeiten um die 320 km/h. Fragen Sie sich, ob Sie im Falle eines Unglücks Zeit zu reagieren und zu fliehen hätten. Lautet die Antwort nein, befinden Sie sich wahrscheinlich an einer unsicheren Stelle.
- Im Interesse der Sicherheit der Zuschauer haben die Veranstalter in bestimmten Bereichen an der Strecke Schilder mit der Aufschrift „Restricted Area" (gesperrter Bereich) oder „Prohibited Area" (Zutrittsverbot) aufgestellt. Dadurch werden ggf. Bereiche gesperrt, an denen Sie zuvor noch zuschauen konnten. Befolgen Sie die Anweisungen der Ordner und suchen Sie sich eine andere Stelle zum Zusehen. Auf einer 60 km langen Strecke gibt es genügend Auswahl!
- Betreten Sie die Straßen nicht mehr, sobald sie gesperrt wurden. Das Betreten oder Eindringen auf eine gesperrte Straße kann eine Anklage und eine hohe Geldstrafe von bis zu 2500 £ nach sich ziehen.

Während Sie die Atmosphäre des TT-Festivals genießen, haben Sie vielleicht Appetit auf ein oder zwei Bier. Wenn Sie Alkohol konsumieren setzen Sie sich danach bitte nicht ans Steuer. Lassen Sie ausreichend Zeit vergehen, bis ihr Körper den Alkohol abgebaut hat. Die Strafen für das Fahren unter Alkoholeinfluss sind auf der Isle of Man ähnlich denen in Großbritannien, mit mindestens einem Fahrverbot von zwölf Monaten.

Routes ouvertes et fermées pour la sécurité des visiteurs

La police de l'Île de Man souhaite à tous les visiteurs de l'île de passer un séjour agréable et en toute sécurité au TT Festival.

Une des caractéristiques unique du TT Festival réside dans le fait que le circuit de 37,73 miles est organisé entièrement sur des routes publiques auxquelles le grand public a accès lorsque les routes sont ouvertes. Nous tenons à souligner que actuellement les routes sont entièrement soumises au code de la route en vigueur qui est appliqué de façon stricte de manière à assurer la sécurité des personnes.

La majeure partie de la législation sur le trafic des routes de l'Île de Man est identique à celle du Royaume-Uni et l'ignorance de la loi ne peut être invoquée comme défense.

À cet effet, veuillez :

Sur routes ouvertes :

- Observer toutes les limitations de vitesse et signalisations.
- Rouler dans ces conditions.
- Rouler ou conduire en fonction de votre propre capacité. C'est particulièrement important en roulant avec des amis ou en groupe.
- Veuillez vous rappeler que ce sont des routes publiques et qu'elles sont empruntées par l'ensemble du grand public, par les agriculteurs également, etc. Tenez compte du fait que des machines agricoles ou autres véhicules lents peuvent se trouver tous proches. Prévoyez l'imprévisible !
- Préparez-vous à faire la queue aux ronds points et intersections lorsque le trafic sur les routes est le plus dense.
- Assurez-vous dans les virages à droite que vous et la machine se trouvent entièrement de votre côté par rapport à la ligne médiane et pas seulement les pneus.
- Le Festival de TT attirent des visiteurs provenant du monde entier, beaucoup d'entre eux ne connaissent pas la conduite à gauche sur la route. Dans cet esprit, veuillez également faire preuve de prudence aux abords de zones de séjour telles que des campings.

Certaines interdictions de circulation instaurées par la Cour de l'Île de Man sont applicables également au Royaume-Uni étant donné qu'il existe à présent un accord réciproque d'interdiction en vigueur, si bien qu'un moment d'égarement sur les routes de l'île pourrait vous coûter cher à long terme.

Aux courses :

- La course TT Races est l'un des sports qui attire le plus grand nombre de spectateur au monde. Nulle part ailleurs vous pouvez être au plus près de l'action assis sur une haie de l'Île de Man entourée d'un paysage à couper le souffle lorsque les meilleurs pilotes de moto sur route au monde vous passent devant.
- Néanmoins, les spectateurs des courses TT sont responsables d'eux-mêmes, du service d'ordre et des pilotes pour assister aux courses d'une manière responsable. Le sport automobile est dangereux et si les organisateurs admettent le fait que vous vouliez être au plus près de l'action vous devez toutefois suivre les règles. En cas de doute, adressez-vous au service d'ordre du site, sa mission est de protéger les pilotes et les spectateurs.
- Choisissez soigneusement votre place et tenez-compte de votre propre sécurité. La place à la meilleure vue n'est pas nécessairement la plus sécurisée. Une moto circulant à 100 mph soit 44 mètres pas seconde peut atteindre une vitesse de 200 mph sur les tronçons les plus rapides de la course. Si malheureusement quelque chose a mal tourné, demandez-vous – « Aurais eu-je le temps de réagir et de bouger ? » Si la réponse est non, vous vous trouvez probablement à une place dangereuse.
- Dans l'intérêt du spectateur, vous verrez que les organisateurs ont marqué certains sites situés autour du circuit avec les marqueurs « Zone réglementée » ou « Zone interdite ». Par conséquent, des zones que vous auriez peut-être vues auparavant peuvent être désormais interdites. Vous devez respecter les conseils du service d'ordre et chercher un autre point de vue. Avec une voie ferrée s'étendant sur plus de 37 miles, vous n'avez que l'embarras du choix !
- Dès que les routes sont fermées, ne les empruntez plus. Marcher ou s'engager sur une route fermée pourrait donner lieu à des poursuites et est passible d'une amende allant jusqu'à £2 500.

Pour finir, vous pouvez, si ça vous plaît, boire une bière ou deux en vous imprégnant de l'atmosphère du Festival TT. Veuillez ne pas conduire sous l'emprise de l'alcool. Attendez suffisamment de temps pour descendre en dessous du seuil d'alcoolémie. Les sanctions pénales en cas de conduite avec un taux supérieur à la limite permise sur l'Île de Man sont les mêmes que celles du Royaume-Uni, à savoir un retrait de permis de conduire minimum d'un an.

Apertura/cierre de carreteras y seguridad de los visitantes

La policía de la Isla de Man desea a todas aquellas personas que asisten al TT Festival que disfruten de una estancia segura y placentera.

Una de las singularidades del TT Festival es que el circuito (37,73 millas) está íntegramente formado por vías públicas por las que circula la población cuando permanecen abiertas. Es importante recalcar que en esas ocasiones las carreteras están totalmente sujetas a la ley sobre tráfico, que se aplica con total firmeza a fin de salvaguardar la seguridad de las personas.

La mayor parte de la legislación sobre tráfico de la Isla de Man coincide con la del Reino Unido, y en tal virtud la ignorancia de la ley no exime de su cumplimiento.

Por ello, cumpla las siguientes normas:
En carreteras abiertas al tráfico:
* Respete los límites de velocidad y las señales.
* Adapte su conducción a las condiciones existentes.
* Conduzca siempre dentro de sus capacidades. Esto es especialmente importante cuando salga en moto con amigos o en grupo.
* Recuerde que circula por vías públicas utilizadas por toda la población, incluyendo granjeros, etc. Tenga presente que puede encontrarse con tractores agrícolas o cualquier otro vehículo lento a la vuelta de cualquier esquina. Esté preparado ante cualquier imprevisto.
* Dado el elevado tráfico en las carreteras, esté preparado para encontrarse colas en rotondas e intersecciones.
* Asegúrese de que tanto sus neumáticos como su cuerpo y su moto se encuentren totalmente en su lado de la línea central de la carretera.
* El TT Festival atrae a visitantes procedentes de muy distintos lugares del mundo y muchos de ellos no están acostumbrados a conducir por el lado izquierdo de la carretera. Teniendo esto presente, extreme las precauciones cuando se aproxime a posibles puntos de inicio de desplazamientos, como es el caso de los campings.

Las prohibiciones de circular impuestas por los tribunales de la Isla de Man son aplicables también en el Reino Unido en virtud del acuerdo de reciprocidad suscrito por ambas partes. Cualquier irresponsabilidad en las carreteras de la isla puede costarle muy caro a largo plazo.

En las carreras:
* Las TT Races son una de las competiciones deportivas con mayor número de espectadores del mundo. En ningún otro lugar se siente tan de cerca la emoción de las dos ruedas; en la Isla de Man podrá sentarse junto a un seto, rodeado de imponentes paisajes, y ver pasar a los principales pilotos de carreras urbanas del mundo.
* No obstante, los espectadores del TT tienen una responsabilidad hacia sí mismos, los comisarios y los pilotos: disfrutar de las carreras de forma responsable. Los deportes de motor entrañan peligros; si bien los organizadores son conscientes de que los espectadores desean estar lo más cerca posible de la acción, es imperativo que se respeten las normas. Si tiene cualquier duda, póngase en contacto con los comisarios que se encuentren en la zona; una de sus funciones es velar por la seguridad de pilotos y espectadores.
* Elija su posición cuidadosamente y tenga presente su seguridad. Es posible que la posición con mejores vistas no sea la más segura. Las motos a 100 mi/h recorren más de 44 metros por segundo y en los tramos más rápidos llegan a alcanzar velocidades del orden de 200 mi/h. Si, por un infortunio, algo saliese mal, hágase la siguiente pregunta: "¿Hubiera tenido tiempo de reaccionar y moverme?" Si su respuesta es negativa, entonces es probable que el sitio elegido no cuente con garantías de seguridad.
* En aras de la seguridad, comprobará cómo los organizadores han señalizado determinadas áreas del circuito con las indicaciones "Zona restringida" o "Zona prohibida". Es posible que algunas zonas desde las que ha disfrutado previamente de la competición se encuentren ahora prohibidas. Respete en todo momento las instrucciones facilitadas por los comisarios y busque posiciones alternativas. Considerando que el trazado supera las 37 millas, seguro que encuentra muchos otros puntos donde instalarse.
* No acceda a las carreteras una vez que estén cerradas. Acceder a carreteras cerradas o caminar por las mismas es una infracción perseguida por la ley y sujeta al pago de elevadas multas de hasta 2500 £.

Por último, puede que la atmósfera del TT Festival le despierte la sed y le apetezca tomar un par de cervezas. Absténgase de conducir si piensa consumir bebidas alcohólicas. Deje transcurrir el tiempo necesario para eliminar el alcohol de su organismo. Las multas por superar el límite de velocidad en la Isla de Man son similares a las del Reino Unido y conllevan, como mínimo, una privación del derecho de conducir de doce meses.

TT Grandstand

Interested in becoming a Marshal?

Are you interested in becoming a Marshal on the world famous TT course? It's easier than you think.

You don't need any experience to join us as we'll give you the basic training required before you go out on the course. As a newcomer you won't be left on your own, you will be placed with experienced marshals to learn the ropes.

You don't have to do all of the practice or race sessions, merely do whatever you want to do, and at the location on the circuit that you would like to be.

All we ask is that you are over 16 (16-18 year olds need their parents' signed permission) and that you are reasonably fit. English is essential as you will need to communicate clearly with the other marshals.

For every practice or race session we need approx 520 marshals on duty, and through the 2013 TT fortnight we used 1,750 marshals, all of whom give us their time and support free.

For further information call in at our office at the rear of the TT Grandstand, visit our

website www.iomttma.com, email us on info@iomttma.com or phone 01624 618191.

Spectator Safety & Behaviour Guidelines

PROHIBITED AREAS

No person or vehicle shall during a closure period enter or remain on any area of land specified as a Prohibited Area. The extent of the Prohibited Areas shall be clearly marked and indicated by notices bearing the words 'PROHIBITED AREA'.

Spectators entering these areas may result in the practices or races being stopped and may also face prosecution.

RESTRICTED AREAS

No unauthorised person or vehicle shall during a closure period enter or remain on any land specified as a Restricted Area. The extent of the restricted areas shall be clearly marked and indicated by notices bearing the words 'RESTRICTED AREA'.

Unruly spectators will be dealt with by the police and the practice or race may have to be stopped. Safety will not be compromised.

Sicherheit der Zuschauer und Verhaltensrichtlinien

BEREICHE MIT ZUTRITTSVERBOT

Während der Sperrung dürfen sich keine Personen oder Fahrzeuge in einem Bereich mit Zutrittsverbot aufhalten oder diesen betreten. Die Fläche eines solchen Bereichs ist klar abgegrenzt und durch Schilder mit den Worten „PROHIBITED AREA" gekennzeichnet.

Zuschauer, die einen solchen Bereich betreten, verursachen ggf. eine Unterbrechung der Trainings oder Rennen und müssen mit einer Anklage rechnen.

GESPERRTE BEREICHE

Während der Sperrung dürfen sich keine unbefugten Personen oder Fahrzeuge in einem gesperrten Bereich aufhalten oder diesen betreten. Die Fläche eines gesperrten Bereichs ist klar abgegrenzt und durch Schilder mit den Worten „RESTRICTED AREA" gekennzeichnet.

Zuwiderhandelnde Zuschauer werden der Polizei übergeben und die Trainings oder Rennen müssen ggf. unterbrochen werden. Die Sicherheit wird nicht gefährdet.

Sécurité des spectateurs & code de conduite

ZONES INTERDITES

Interdiction aux personnes et véhicules d'entrer ou de rester dans des zones de l'île considérées comme des zones interdites. L'étendue des zones interdites doit être clairement marquée et indiquée avec la mention « ZONE INTERDITE ».

Si des spectateurs entrent dans ces zones, les essais ou les courses peuvent être interrompus ce qui pourrait faire l'objet d'une poursuite judiciaire.

ZONES REGLEMENTEES

Tous véhicules et personnes non autorisés ne peuvent entrer ou rester dans des zones de l'île considérées comme des zones réglementées. L'étendue des zones réglementées doit être clairement marquée et indiquée avec la mention « ZONE REGLEMENTEE ».

Les spectateurs indisciplinés seront renvoyés par la police et les essais ou la course pourraient être interrompus. La sécurité ne doit jamais être compromise.

Directrices sobre seguridad y comportamiento de los espectadores

ZONAS PROHIBIDAS

Está prohibido el acceso o estancia de personas o vehículos en cualquiera de los lugares especificados como zonas prohibidas durante el tiempo que se mantenga el cierre de carreteras. Las zonas prohibidas están claramente señalizadas e indicadas mediante letreros con las palabras "ZONA PROHIBIDA" (PROHIBITED AREA).

El acceso de los espectadores a estas zonas puede provocar la interrupción de los entrenamientos o de las propias carreras, motivo por el que los infractores pueden ser procesados.

ZONAS RESTRINGIDAS

Está prohibido el acceso o estancia de personas o vehículos no autorizados en cualquiera de los lugares especificados como zonas restringidas durante el tiempo que se mantenga el cierre de carreteras. Las zonas restringidas están claramente señalizadas e indicadas mediante letreros con las palabras "ZONA RESTRINGIDA" (RESTRICTED AREA).

El acceso de los espectadores a estas zonas puede provocar la interrupción de los entrenamientos o de las propias carreras, motivo por el que los infractores responder ante la policía. La seguridad no debe verse comprometida bajo ningún concepto.

Advice and information

Banks and Bank Holidays
Most high street banks and building societies have premises on the Isle of Man. Opening hours are generally 9.30am to 4.30pm. Bank Holidays are the same as those in England with two additional holidays. Senior Race Day (TT Races) is Friday of Race Week and Tynwald Day (Manx National Day) is celebrated on 5th July unless it falls on a weekend.

Car Hire
There are several car hire companies on the Island. Clean driving licences are required. Driving in the Isle of Man is on the left, as in the UK; seatbelts must be worn and the Horse Trams that run up and down Douglas promenade can only be overtaken on the left. It is illegal to drive any vehicle whilst using your mobile phone.

Car Parking
Free parking is available in designated spaces in all main towns; however, there is a time limit to how long you can stay. Parking Discs must be displayed in the windscreen showing the time you arrived. These discs are widely available – your hotel may have a supply but if not you can obtain them from the Welcome Centre at the Sea Terminal in Douglas, or on the Steam Packet ferries. Hire companies will provide these in each car.

Cash Machines
Automated cash machines are available in all the major towns around the Isle of Man. Isle of Man bank notes are dispensed from all cash machines apart from those situated at the Sea Terminal and the Airport, where English notes are issued.

Chemists
Dispensing chemists are open from 9.00am to 5.30pm Mondays to Saturdays. Outside of these times there are limited opening hours and a duty chemist rota is in operation. This list can be obtained from the Department of Health prior to travel. Alternatively, these are posted in the local press and your hotel should be able to provide you with details. Duty Rota hours are from 5.30pm to 6.30pm Mon – Fri (excluding Bank Holidays) and Sundays and Bank Holidays from 12noon to 1.00pm.

Currency Information
The Isle of Man has its own currency with the same denominations as the UK and still has £1 notes. UK currency is legal tender in the Isle of Man but Manx currency is not accepted in the UK, although notes can be exchanged at UK banks.

Doctors and Hospitals
The Manx Emergency Doctor Service (MEDS) operates an 'Out of Hours' emergency service when doctors' surgeries are closed. The service is contactable on +44(0) 1624 650355 and is ONLY available from 6.00pm to 8.00am Monday to Friday, with 24-hour cover over weekends and Bank Holidays.

In an emergency please attend A&E (telephone +44 (0) 1624 650040 for A&E). For life threatening emergencies call emergency services on 999.

The Isle of Man Nobles Hospital is just outside Douglas at The Strang, Braddan, telephone +44 (0) 1624 650000 (24 hrs).

Ramsey Cottage Hospital, telephone +44 (0) 1624 811811 for general enquiries (0800-2000 hours).

RECIPROCAL HEALTH AGREEMENT:

UK residents visiting the Isle of Man receive free NHS treatment if they become ill. Statutory charges (e.g. prescription charges) are applicable for both residents and visitors. It is strongly **recommended that all visitors ensure they have appropriate insurance** in place which will cover repatriation to the UK by air ambulance if necessary. Information regarding the Reciprocal Agreement is correct at the time of publication but visitors should check prior to their visit.

Identification and passports

Passports are not required to enter the Isle of Man if you are travelling from the UK or Ireland although airlines require some form of photographic identification. European and global travellers have to clear customs and passport control on arrival in the UK or Ireland before travelling on to the Isle of Man. A night at the Casino requires photographic identification.

Mobile Phones

There are two mobile phone networks operating on the Isle of Man – Manx Telecom and Sure. Each mobile network has commercial agreements with mobile phone networks in the UK, Europe and the rest of the world and it is advisable to check with your own mobile network to determine the level and charges of roaming services with Isle of Man providers. Please note the Isle of Man is outside the EU jurisdiction and does not benefit from the tariff caps operating within the European Union.

Police

Isle of Man Police are easily recognisable and are very approachable should you need assistance.

Police Headquarters, Glencrutchery Road, Douglas, telephone +44 (0) 1624 631212. In an emergency please dial 999.

Taxis

Taxi ranks are outside the entrance of the Sea Terminal and airport buildings. Taxis are available to meet flights and sailings and most destinations are covered by fixed tariff charges.

Weather and Shipping Forecasts

Up-to-date forecasts are provided by the Ronaldsway Met Office:

- Recorded weather forecast: 0900 624 3300 (Premium rate)
- Weatherman – 24 hours: 0900 624 3200 (Premium rate)
- Recorded shipping forecast: 0900 624 3322 (Premium rate)

Online Information

www.gov.im/infocentre
www.bbc.co.uk/weather/3042237

Hinweise und informationEN

Banken und gesetzliche Feiertage

Die meisten internationalen Banken und Bausparkassen verfügen über Filialen auf der Isle of Man. Die Öffnungszeiten sind in der Regel von 9.30 Uhr bis 16.30 Uhr. Es gibt dieselben gesetzlichen Feiertage wie in England und zwei zusätzliche Feiertage. Dabei handelt es sich um den Senior Race Day (TT-Rennen), der am Freitag der Rennwoche gefeiert wird, und um den Tynwald Day (Nationalfeiertag), der am 5. Juli gefeiert wird, sofern er nicht auf ein Wochenende fällt.

Autovermietungen

Auf der Insel gibt es mehrere Autovermietungen. Es muss ein gültiger Führerschein vorgelegt werden. Auf der Isle of Man gilt Linksverkehr wie im Vereinigten Königreich, es besteht Gurtpflicht und die Pferdegespanne auf der Promenade in Douglas dürfen nur links überholt werden. Während des Führens von Fahrzeugen dürfen keine Handys benutzt werden.

Parken

In allen größeren Städten gibt es auf den ausgewiesenen Flächen kostenlose Parkplätze. Allerdings besteht eine zeitliche Beschränkung. In der Windschutzscheibe sind Parkscheiben zu platzieren, auf denen die Ankunftszeit eingestellt wird. Solche Parkscheiben sind leicht erhältlich – unter Umständen sind sie sogar in Ihrem Hotel verfügbar. Andernfalls sind sie am Informationszentrum des Meeresbahnhofs in Douglas und auf den Steam-Packet-Fähren erhältlich. Autovermietungen stellen mit dem Mietwagen auch Parkscheiben bereit.

Geldautomaten

Geldautomaten gibt es in allen größeren Städten auf der Isle of Man. Alle Geldautomaten geben Banknoten der Isle of Man aus, ausgenommen sind die Geldautomaten am Meeresbahnhof und am Flughafen, die englische Banknoten ausgeben.

Apotheken

Apotheken sind montags bis samstags von 9.00 Uhr bis 17.30 Uhr geöffnet. Außerhalb dieser Zeit gibt es begrenzte Öffnungszeiten und einen Sonderdienstplan. Eine Liste kann vor der Reise beim Department of Health (Gesundheitsministerium) angefordert werden. Außerdem werden diese Informationen in der Lokalpresse veröffentlicht und Ihr Hotel kann Ihnen ebenfalls weiterhelfen. Die Sonderdienstzeiten sind Mo-Fr von 17.30 Uhr bis 18.30 Uhr (außer an Feiertagen) und sonntags sowie an Feiertagen von 12.00 Uhr bis 13.00 Uhr.

Währungsinformationen

Die Isle of Man hat eine eigene Währung mit derselben Unterteilung wie im Vereinigten Königreich und es werden noch 1£-Scheine verwendet. Das britische Pfund ist ein gesetzliches Zahlungsmittel auf der Isle of Man, umgekehrt werden Isle-of-Man-Pfund jedoch nicht im Vereinigten Königreich akzeptiert, können aber umgetauscht werden.

Ärzte und Krankenhäuser

Der Notarztdienst MEDS (Manx Emergency Doctor Service) stellt einen Notdienst außerhalb der Öffnungszeiten der Arztpraxen bereit. Der Notdienst ist telefonisch unter der Nummer +44(0) 1624 650355 von Montag bis Freitag NUR von 18.00 Uhr bis 8.00 Uhr und an Wochenenden und Feiertagen rund um die Uhr erreichbar.

Besuchen Sie in Notfällen bitte die Notaufnahme (Telefon: +44 (0) 1624 650040). Bei lebensbedrohlichen Notfällen rufen Sie bitte den Rettungsdienst unter der Nummer 999.

Das Krankenhaus „Isle of Man Nobles Hospital" befindet sich außerhalb von Douglas in The Strang, Braddan. Telefon: +44 (0) 1624 650000 (rund um die

THE HIDDEN GEM OF THE ISLE OF MAN.

The Abbey is set in green and luscious surroundings with mature trees, a babbling stream and an ancient monastery for company.
Our restaurant offers unique and interesting tastes of fresh food cooked to perfection for your enjoyment.
Our large dining room has a daily changing menu of seasonal produce in the tradition of modern European.
Outstanding and interesting wine list predominantly sourced from France, Spain and Italy.

• SPECIAL CLUB LUNCHEON MENU FROM 12.00PM • AMPLE PARKING
• OPEN WEDNESDAY-SUNDAY • AFTERNOON TEA FROM 2.30

Rushen Abbey, Ballasalla, Isle of Man IM9 3DB
01624 822393 • www.theabbey.im

THE ABBEY
RESTAURANT

SMOKEHOUSE, GRILL AND BAR.
PARTY TENT, OUTDOOR DECK AND THE WILDS.

Open 7 days a week from Easter • Food served 12noon-9.30pm • No booking necessary

The Forge, Santon, Isle of Man IM4 1JE
01624 610031 • www.theforge.im

THE FORGE

Racing on the Mountain

Uhr). Bei allgemeinen Fragen wenden Sie sich an das „Cottage Hospital" in Ramsey, Telefon: +44 (0) 1624 811811 (von 8.00 bis 20.00 Uhr).

GEGENSEITIGES GESUNDHEITSABKOMMEN:
Bürger des Vereinigten Königreichs, die die Isle of Man besuchen, erhalten im Krankheitsfall eine kostenlose Behandlung gemäß NHS. Gesetzliche Kosten (z. B. Rezeptgebühren) fallen für Einwohner und Besucher an. Alle Besucher müssen sicherstellen, dass sie über eine angemessene Krankenversicherung verfügen, die ggf. auch einen Transport in die Heimat per Flugzeug abdeckt. Die Informationen zum Gesundheitsabkommen entsprechen dem Stand zum Zeitpunkt der Veröffentlichung. Besucher sollten diese vor der Reise prüfen.

Ausweis und Pass

Besucher aus dem Vereinigten Königreich und Irland benötigen keinen Pass für die Einreise auf die Isle of Man, allerdings verlangen die Fluggesellschaften einen Lichtbildausweis. Besucher aus Europa und anderen Teilen der Welt müssen bei Ankunft im Vereinigten Königreich oder Irland vor der Weiterreise zur Isle of Man die Zollabfertigung und Passkontrolle durchlaufen. Für einen Besuch des Kasinos ist ein Lichtbildausweis vorzulegen.

Mobiltelefone

Auf der Isle of Man sind zwei Mobilfunknetze in Betrieb: Manx Telecom und Sure. Beide haben Vereinbarungen mit Mobilfunknetzen im Vereinigten Königreich, Europa und anderen Teilen der Welt. Erkundigen Sie sich bei Ihrem Anbieter bezüglich der Roaming-Gebühren in Mobilfunknetzen auf der Isle of Man. Beachten Sie, dass die Isle of Man nicht unter die Gesetzgebung der EU fällt und die Tarifdeckelung nicht gilt.

Polizei

Die Polizisten der Isle of Man sind leicht zu erkennen und sehr hilfsbereit, falls Sie Hilfe benötigen.
Polizeipräsidium, Glencrutchery Road, Douglas, Telefon: +44 (0) 1624 631212.
In einer Notsituation wählen Sie bitte 999.

Taxis

Taxistände befinden sich vor dem Eingang des Meeresbahnhofs und der Flughafengebäude. Taxis stehen zur Verfügung, um Flüge und Schiffe zu erreichen. Außerdem sind die meisten Ziele mit festen Tarifen abgedeckt.

Wetter- und Seewettervorhersagen

Aktuelle Vorhersagen liefert das Ronaldsway Met Office:

- Aufgezeichnete Wettervorhersage: 0900 624 3300 (kostenpflichtig)
- Wetteransager rund um die Uhr: 0900 624 3200 (kostenpflichtig)
- Aufgezeichnete Seewettervorhersage: 0900 624 3322 (kostenpflichtig)

Informationen im Internet

www.gov.im/infocentre
www.bbc.co.uk/weather/3042237

Conseils et information

Banques et jours de fermeture des banques

La plupart des établissements bancaires et sociétés d'épargne immobilière disposent de locaux sur l'Île de Man. Les horaires d'ouverture sont généralement de 9h30 à 16h30. Les jours de fermeture des banques sont les mêmes que ceux en Angleterre avec deux jours de fermeture supplémentaires. Le Senior Race Day (TT Races) tombe en juin et le Tynwald Day (le Manx National Day) est célébré le 5 juillet sauf s'il tombe un week-end.

Voiture de location

Il existe plusieurs sociétés de location de voiture sur l'île. Un permis de conduire B est requis. La conduite sur l'Île de Man est à gauche comme dans l'ensemble du Royaume-Uni : les ceintures de sécurité doivent être mises et les trams à chevaux qui montent et descendent la promenade de Douglas peuvent être dépassés uniquement par la gauche. Il est interdit de conduire un véhicule en téléphonant avec un portable.

Aire de stationnement

Le stationnement gratuit est disponible sur des emplacements désignés dans toutes les villes principales ; toutefois, la durée de stationnement est limitée. Les vignettes de stationnement doivent être apposées sur le pare-brise pour montrer l'heure de votre arrivée. Ces vignettes sont disponibles aisément – votre hôtel peut vous en fournir, sinon vous pouvez en obtenir au Centre d'accueil de la gare maritime de Douglas ou sur Steam Packet ferries. Des sociétés de location les prévoient dans chaque voiture.

Distributeurs automatiques

Des distributeurs automatiques de billets se trouvent dans toutes les villes principales situées autour de l'île. Tous les distributeurs automatiques distribuent des billets de banque de l'Île de Man à part ceux situés à la gare maritime et à l'aéroport où des billets anglais sont émis.

Pharmacies

Les pharmacies sont ouvertes de 9h00 à 17h30 du lundi au samedi. En dehors de cette plage, une pharmacie de garde est ouverte avec des horaires restreints. Vous pouvez demander une liste auprès du Ministère de la santé avant votre départ. Autrement, ils sont publiés dans la presse locale et votre hôtel devrait être en mesure de vous les fournir en détail. Les heures de garde sont de 17h30 à 6h30 du lundi au vendredi (sauf les jours de fermeture des banques) et le samedi et les jours de fermeture des banques de 12h00 à 13h00.

Information sur la devise

L'Île de Man possède sa propre monnaie avec les mêmes coupures que celles du Royaume-Uni et a encore des billets de £1. La Livre anglaise a cours légal sur l'Île de Man mais la monnaie mannoise n'est pas acceptée au Royaume-Uni, bien que les billets puissent être échangés par les banques.

Médecins et hôpitaux

Le Manx Emergency Doctor Service (MEDS) gère un service d'urgence qui est ouvert en dehors des horaires habituels lorsque les cabinets médicaux sont fermés. Le service est joignable au +44(0) 1624 650355 et est disponible UNIQUEMENT de 18h00 à 8h00 du lundi au vendredi, une garde de 24 heures pendant les weekends et les jours de fermeture des banques. En cas d'urgence, veuillez vous présenter au A&E (téléphone +44 (0) 1624 650040 pour A&E). En cas d'urgence vitale, appelez les services d'urgence au 999. Le Nobles Hospital de l'Île de Man se situe juste à la périphérie de Douglas à The Strang, Braddan. Téléphone +44 (0) 1624 650000 (24 heures). Ramsey Cottage Hospital, téléphone +44 (0) 1624 811811 pour obtenir des renseignements (0800 – 2000 heures).

ACCORD RECIPROQUE SUR LA SANTE : Les résidents du Royaume-Uni visitant l'Île de Man reçoivent des soins du NHS s'ils devaient tomber malades. Les prélèvements obligatoires (les prescriptions de prise en charge, par ex.) s'appliquent aux résidents et aux visiteurs. Il est vivement recommandé à tous les visiteurs de s'assurer qu'ils ont souscrit une assurance suffisante en vigueur qui couvrira, si nécessaire, le rapatriement au Royaume-Uni par ambulance aérienne. Les informations concernant l'Accord réciproque est exact au moment de sa publication. Toutefois, les visiteurs devraient vérifier avant de venir.

Identification et passeports
Les passeports ne sont pas requis pour rentrer sur le territoire de l'Île de Man si vous voyagez en provenance du Royaume-Uni ou de l'Irlande. Toutefois, les aéroports demandent une pièce d'identité avec photo. Les voyageurs européens et internationaux doivent passer la douane et le contrôle des passeports à leur arrivée au Royaume-Uni ou en Irlande avant de venir sur l'Île de Man. Une pièce d'identité avec photo est demandée pour passer une soirée au casino.

Téléphones portables
Il existe deux réseaux de téléphonie mobile exploités sur l'Île de Man – Manx Telecom and Sure. Chacun des réseaux de téléphonie mobile a conclu des accords commerciaux avec les réseaux de téléphonie mobile du Royaume-Uni, d'Europe et du monde et il est recommandé de vérifier avec votre propre réseau de téléphonie mobile afin de déterminer le niveau et la couverture des services de données en itinérance avec les opérateurs de l'Île de Man. Veuillez noter que l'Île de Man n'est pas sous le joug de la juridiction de l'UE et ne bénéficie pas de plafonnements tarifaires instaurés au sein de l'Union européenne.

Police
La police de l'Île de Man est facilement reconnaissable et est très appréciable si vous deviez rencontrer des difficultés.
Quartier général de police, Glencrutchery Road, Douglas, téléphone +44 (0) 1624 631212.
En cas d'urgence, veuillez composer le 999

Taxis
Les stations de taxis se trouvent à l'extérieur de l'entrée de la gare maritime et des bâtiments aéroportuaires. Des taxis sont disponibles pour rejoindre des vols et dessertes, et la plupart des destinations sont desservies par des tarifs fixes.

Prévisions météorologiques et météo-marée
Les mises à jour des prévisions sont disponibles auprès du service météorologique de Ronaldsway.
- Prévisions météorologiques enregistrées : 0900 624 3300 (taux majoré)
- Présentateur(trice) météo – 24h/24 : 0900 624 3200 (taux majoré)
- Météo-marée enregistrée : 0900 624 3322 (taux majoré)

Informations en ligne
www.gov.im/infocentre
www.bbc.co.uk/weather/3042237

Consejos e información

Oficinas bancarias y días festivos

La Isla de Man cuenta con sucursales de las principales instituciones bancarias y cajas de ahorros. Su horario de apertura es generalmente de 9.30 a 16.30 horas. Los festivos son los mismos que en Inglaterra, a los que hay que añadir dos días adicionales. Estos son el Senior Race Day (TT Races), celebrado el viernes de la semana de competición, y el Tynwald Day (el Manx National Day), que se celebra el 5 de julio salvo que ese día caiga en fin de semana.

Alquiler de coches

La isla dispone de varias empresas de alquiler de coches. Para poder alquilar un vehículo es necesario contar con un permiso de conducción sin infracciones. En la Isla de Man se conduce por la izquierda, al igual que en el Reino Unido; el uso de los cinturones de seguridad es obligatorio y únicamente puede adelantarse a los tranvías tirados por caballos que ascienden y descienden el paseo de Douglas por la izquierda. Está prohibido el uso de teléfonos móviles mientras se conduce.

Aparcamiento

Existen aparcamientos gratuitos en zonas designadas de las principales localidades de la isla; no obstante, existe un límite temporal en cuanto a la permanencia en estas plazas. Las tarjetas de aparcamiento deben colocarse en el parabrisas e indicar la hora de llegada. Estas tarjetas son fáciles de conseguir. Su propio hotel puede proporcionárselas; si su hotel carece de ellas, puede obtenerlas en el centro de visitantes de la terminal marítima de Douglas o bien en los ferris de la compañía Steam Packet. Las empresas de alquiler de coches incluyen las tarjetas en todos sus vehículos.

Cajeros automáticos

Encontrará cajeros automáticos en las principales localidades de la Isla de Man. Todos los cajeros automáticos dispensan billetes de la Isla de Man, con excepción de aquellos situados en la terminal marítima y el aeropuerto que únicamente ofrecen billetes del Reino Unido.

Farmacias

Las farmacias permanecen abiertas de 9.00 a 17.30 horas de lunes a sábado. Existen farmacias de guardia fuera de este horario habitual. Puede solicitar una lista con las farmacias de guardia al Departamento de Salud antes de iniciar su viaje. También encontrará información sobre las farmacias de guardia en la prensa local; su hotel podrán facilitarle seguramente información a este respecto. Los horarios de las farmacias de guardia son de 17.30 a 18.30 horas de lunes a viernes (excepto festivos) y de 12.00 del mediodía a 13.00 horas los domingos y festivos.

Moneda

La Isla de Man tiene su propia divisa con idénticas denominaciones que en el Reino Unido (además de billetes de 1 £). La libra esterlina es moneda de curso legal en la Isla de Man; por el contrario, la divisa insular no se acepta en el Reino Unido. No obstante, sí pueden cambiarse billetes en las entidades bancarias del Reino Unido.

Médicos y hospitales

El Manx Emergency Doctor Service (MEDS) cuenta con un servicio de urgencias "fuera de horario" para atender a pacientes cuando las consultas médicas están cerradas. Puede contactar con este servicio llamando al teléfono +44(0) 1624 650355. Recuerde que este servicio ÚNICAMENTE está disponible de lunes a viernes, de 6 de la tarde a 8 de la mañana, y las 24 horas del día los fines de semana y festivos.

En caso de urgencia acuda por favor al servicio de

urgencias (teléfono +44 (0) 1624 650040 para urgencias). En caso de urgencia con riesgo de muerte llame al teléfono 999 (servicio de urgencias). El Nobles Hospital de la Isla de Man se encuentra en las afueras de Douglas en The Strang, Braddan. Teléfono +44 (0) 1624 650000 (24 horas). Ramsey Cottage Hospital: teléfono para consultas generales +44 (0) 1624 811811 (08.00 - 20.00 horas).

CONVENIO RECÍPROCO DE ASISTENCIA SANITARIA: Los residentes en el Reino Unido que visitan la Isla de Man disfrutan de asistencia sanitaria gratuita por parte del NHS en caso de enfermedad. Tanto los residentes como los visitantes deben sufragar obligatoriamente una serie de costes (por ejemplo, los gastos por recetas). Se recomienda encarecidamente a todos los visitantes que comprueben si sus seguros médicos cubren la repatriación al Reino Unido en ambulancia aérea en caso de necesidad. La información relativa al Convenio Recíproco de Asistencia Sanitaria es correcta en el momento de su publicación; no obstante, se insta a los visitantes a comprobar la misma antes de su visita.

Identificación y pasaportes

No es necesario el pasaporte para entrar en la Isla de Man si viaja desde el Reino Unido o Irlanda; no obstante, algunas compañías aéreas exigen algún tipo de identificación fotográfica. Los visitantes procedentes del resto de Europa o del mundo deben pasar un control de aduanas y pasaportes a su llegada al Reino Unido o Irlanda antes de poder viajar a la Isla de Man. Para poder acceder al casino se requiere mostrar alguna forma de identificación fotográfica.

Teléfonos móviles

La Isla de Man cuenta con dos operadores de telefonía móvil: Manx Telecom y Sure. Ambos operadores tienen suscritos acuerdos comerciales con los operadores de telefonía móvil del Reino Unido, del resto de Europa y del mundo; es aconsejable consultar a su propio operador móvil la disponibilidad del servicio de itinerancia y el coste del mismo en la Isla de Man. Tenga presente que la Isla de Man no está dentro de la jurisdicción de la UE y, en consecuencia, no se beneficia de los límites de tarifas aplicables en la Unión Europea.

Policía

Los miembros de la policía de la Isla de Man son fácilmente reconocibles y muy accesibles en caso de requerirse su asistencia. Jefatura de policía, Glencrutchery Road, Douglas, teléfono +44 (0) 1624 631212. Llame al 999 en caso de producirse una emergencia.

Taxis

Las paradas de taxi se localizan en el exterior de la entrada de la terminal marítima y del aeropuerto. Los taxis dan servicio al aeropuerto y la terminal marítima; la mayoría de los destinos tienen una tarifa fija.

Previsiones meteorológicas y sobre el estado del mar

El centro meteorológico Ronaldsway Met Office proporciona previsiones actualizadas:
- Previsiones meteorológicas grabadas: 0900 624 3300 (tarificación especial)
- Meteorólogo (24 horas): 0900 624 3200 (tarificación especial)
- Previsiones grabadas sobre el estado del mar: 0900 624 3322 (tarificación especial)

Información en línea

www.gov.im/infocentre
www.bbc.co.uk/weather/3042237

Information
Informationen
Information
Información

PEEL
- **Banks/Banken/Banques/Bancos:**
Isle of Man Bank, Athol St, Peel Tel: 637000
Lloyds TSB Bank, Douglas St, Peel Tel: 08457 301280
- **Chemist/Apotheke/Pharmacie/Farmacia:**
Clear Pharmacy, Michael St, Peel Tel: 843130
Cowley Pharmacy, Atholl Place Tel: 842264
- **Post Office/Post/Poste/Correos:**
Douglas Street, Peel Tel: 842282
Main Road, Foxdale Tel: 801295
Station Road, St Johns Tel: 801225
- **Police Station/Polizei/Police/Policía:**
Derby Rd, Peel Tel: 842208
- **Tourist Information/Touristische Informationen/**
  Informations touristiques/Información turística:
Town Hall, Derby Rd, Peel Tel: 842341
- **Dentist/Zahnarzt/Dentiste/Dentista:**
Hanson Dental Practice, 18 Stanley Rd, Peel Tel: 842412
Westview Dental Practice, Close Beg, Ballawattleworth, Peel Tel: 843311
- **Doctor/Mediziner/Médecin/Médico:**
Peel Medical Centre, Albany Rd, Peel Tel: 686968
- **Taxi:**
Annes Taxi 843799
West Coast Taxis 842889

PORT ERIN, PORT ST MARY, CASTLETOWN, BALLASALLA
- **Banks/Banken/Banques/Bancos:**
Isle of Man Bank, Station Rd, Port Erin Tel: 821420
Isle of Man Bank, Market Sq, Castletown Tel: 821400
Barclays, Market Sq, Castletown Tel: 0845 601 6240
Lloyds TSB Bank, Market Sq, Castletown Tel: 0845 850 1850
- **Chemist/Apotheke/Pharmacie/Farmacia:**
Lloyds Pharmacies, Church Rd, Port Ein Tel: 833101
Clear Pharmacy, Orchard Rd, Port Erin Tel: 832139
Clear Pharmacy, Bay View Road, Port St Mary Tel: 832128
Castle Pharmacy, Malew St., Castletown Tel: 822512
Lloyds Pharmacy, The Parade, Castletown Tel: 823272
Costain Pharmacy, Main Road, Ballasalla Tel: 824793
- **Post Office/Post/Poste/Correos:**
Church Road, Port Erin Tel: 833119

Bay View Road, Port St Mary Tel: 833118
Main Road, Ballasalla Tel: 829526
The Parade, Castletown Tel: 824765
- **Police Station/Polizei/Police/Policía:**
Station Rd, Port Erin Tel: 832222
Castle St, Castletown Tel: 822222
Ballasalla Tel: 822543
- **Tourist Information/Touristische Informationen/**
  Informations touristiques/Información turística:
Port Erin Commissioners, Station Rd Tel: 832298
Port Erin Arts Centre, Victoria Sq Tel: 832662
The Old Grammar School, Castle Rushen (seasonal)
Ronaldsway Airport
- **Dentist/Zahnarzt/Dentiste/Dentista:**
Abbey Dental, 4 Silverburn Drive, Ballasalla Tel: 823040
Port Erin Dental Surgery, Orange Grove Hse, Orchard Rd, Port Erin Tel: 833667
Port St Mary Dental practice, 35 High St, Port St Mary Tel: 833234
- **Doctor/Mediziner/Médecin/Médico:**
Ballasalla Medical Centre, Main Rd, Ballasalla Tel: 823243
Castletown Medical Centre, Sandfield, Castletoen Tel: 686939
Southern Group Practice, Castletown Rd, Port Erin Tel: 686979
- **Taxi:**
Bunty's Taxis 835433 or 07624 493652
K-Force Taxis 07624 472616
Associated Castletown & Airport Taxis 825757

RAMSEY
- **Banks/Banken/Banques/Bancos:**
Barclays, Parliament St, Ramsey Tel: 684684
Isle of Man, Parliament St, Ramsey Tel: 811200
Lloyds TSB, Parliament St, Ramsey Tel: 0845 730 1280
HSBC, St Paul's Sq, Ramsey Tel: 0845 600 6161
- **Chemist/Apotheke/Pharmacie/Farmacia:**
Lloyds Pharmacies:
17 Parliament St, Ramsey Tel: 812167
Shoprite Store, Bowring Rd, Ramsey Tel: 812246
6 St Pauls Sq, Ramsey Tel: 814388
Kirk Michael Village Pharmacy, Main Rd Tel: 878545
- **Post Office/Post/Poste/Correos:**
Parliament St, Ramsey Tel: 812248

Main Road, Ballaugh Tel: 896081
School Close, Jurby Tel: 897555
Andreas Village Shop, Andreas Tel: 880303
Main Road, Kirk Michael Tel: 878226
Main Road, Sulby Tel: 897205
- **Police Station/Polizei/Police/Policía:**
Ramsey Town Hall, Ramsey Tel: 812234
Kirk Michael, Tel: 878228
Andreas, Tel: 880212
- **Tourist Information/Touristische Informationen/
Informations touristiques/Información turística:**
Ramsey Library Tel: 810146
- **Dentist/Zahnarzt/Dentiste/Dentista:**
Grove Mount Dental Practice, Grove Mount South, Ramsey Tel: 812157
- **Doctor/Mediziner/Médecin/Médico:**
Ramsey Group Practice, Grove Mount, Ramsey Tel: 813881
- **Taxi:**
Ramsey Taxis 818181
Andreas Taxis 07624 300500
Ayres Taxis 818118
Island Taxis 878878
Kirk Michael Taxis 878787
Lezayre Taxis Service 07624 429111
Manx Taxis 817788

DOUGLAS, ONCHAN, LAXEY
- **Banks/Banken/Banques/Bancos:**
Barclays Bank, Barclays Ho, Victoria St Tel: 0845 601 6240
Isle of Man Bank, Athol St, Douglas Tel: 632330, Prospect Terr, Douglas Tel: 632330 & Regent St, Douglas Tel: 632310
Lloyds TSB Bank, Victoria House, Prospect Hill, Douglas Tel: 0845 850 1850
HSBC Bank, Ridgeway St, Douglas Tel: 0845 600 6161
NatWest Bank, Ridgeway Street, Douglas Tel: 632350
- **Chemist/Apotheke/Pharmacie/Farmacia:**
Clear Pharmacy, 13 Castle St Tel: 673402
Boots the Chemist, 14–22 Strand St Tel: 616120
Hemensley's Pharmacy, 1 Windsor Rd Tel: 675162
Kinrade Pharmacy, Ballaquayle Rd, Douglas Tel: 673912
Lloyd Pharmacy, Shoprite, Victoria Rd, Douglas Tel: 673268
Corkills Pharmacy, 1 Main Road, Onchan Tel: 615150
Lloyds Pharmacy, 18b–21b Village Walk, Onchan Tel: 676410
Rodan S C Pharmacy, 15 New Road, Laxey Tel: 861221
- **Post Office/Post/Poste/Correos:**
Anagh Coar, Cudhag Road, Douglas Tel: 613457
Governors Hill, Hailwood Av e, Onchan Tel: 667958
Regent St, Douglas Tel: 686141
Crosby Ter, Douglas Tel: 675027
Saddlestone Stores, Ballaughton Lane, Douglas Tel: 623438
Main Road, Onchan Tel: 676031
Port Jack, Onchan Tel: 612567
New Rd, Laxey Tel: 861209

Main Rd, Union Mills Tel: 852690
- **Police Station/Polizei/Police/Policía:**
Police H.Q., Duke Ave, Douglas Tel: 631212
Laxey Tel: 861210
- **Tourist Information/Touristische Informationen/
Informations touristiques/Información turística:**
The Welcome Centre, Sea Terminal Tel: 686766 (All Island/Open all year).
The Library, Willow House, Main Rd Tel: 621228
- **Dentist/Zahnarzt/Dentiste/Dentista:**
Woodbourne Dental Surgery, 65 Woodbourne Rd, Douglas Tel: 675164
Tracey Bell Super Clinic, Kensington Rd, Douglas Tel: 613323
Mann Dental Care, 34 Kensington Rd Tel: 673429
Smithson & Jones, 12 Hilary Rd, Douglas Tel: 675195
A D Hewett Dental Practice, 84 Bucks Rd, Douglas Tel: 675748
Avondale Dental Practice, 3 Avondale Court, Onchan Tel: 624620
Compass Dental Surgery, The Village Walk, Onchan Tel: 622837
Laxey Dental Surgery, 39 New Rd, Laxey Tel: 863422
- **Doctor/Mediziner/Médecin/Médico:**
Promenade Medical Centre, Level 2, Chester St Car Park,Douglas Tel: 675490
Kensington Health Centre, West Moreland Rd, Douglas Tel: 642333
Palatine Group Practice, Palatine Health Centre, Strang Corner Field, Braddan Tel: 623931
Hailwood Medical Centre, 2 Hailwood Ct, Governors Hill, Douglas Tel: 686949
Laxey Health Centre, New Rd, Laxey Tel: 861350
Village Walk Health Centre, 1 Village Walk, Onchan Tel: 656020
- **Taxi:**
A1 Taxi Group Tel: 674488
Douglas Taxis Tel: 623623
Phil Cowin Taxis Tel: 620205
Telecabs Tel: 629191
Laxy Cabs 07624 432343
- **Car Hire/Autovermietung/Location de voitures/Renta de autos:**
Mylchreests Car Rental, Ronaldsway Airport, Ballasalla Tel: 08000 190335
Ocean Ford, Airport Tel: 820830

🇬🇧 Free WiFi **Hotspots**

Wi-Fi access is readily available on the Island at the Sea Terminal,
Ronaldsway Airport, Local libraries and many cafes and hotels.

🇩🇪 Ksotenlose WLAN **Hotspots**

WLAN steht am Meeresbahnhof, Flughafen Ronaldsway, in Bibliotheken sowie in vielen Cafés
und Hotels bereit.

🇫🇷 **Bornes e'accés** WiFi Gratuites

L'accès WiFi s'obtient facilement à la gare maritime de l'île, à l'aéroport de Ronaldsway, dans les
librairies locales et dans les nombreux cafés et hôtels.

🇪🇸 **Puntos** WiFi Gratuitos

La isla cuenta con puntos Wi-Fi fácilmente disponibles en la terminal marítima, el aeropuerto
de Ronaldsway, las bibliotecas y en muchas cafeterías y hoteles.

m: manx telecon

- *North/Nord/Nord/Norte:*
Barista Coffee House, Ramsey
Bar Logo, Ramsey
Costa, Ramsey
Mooragh Park Cafe, Ramsey
Trafalgar Hotel, Ramsey
- *West/West/Ouest/Oeste:*
Davison's Ice Cream Parlour, Peel
House of Manannan Cafe, Peel
Marine Hotel, Peel
Niarbyl Cafe, Niarbyl
Peel Breakwater Cafe, Peel
Waterfall Countrty Pub, Glen Maye
Greens Restaurant, St Johns
- *East/Ost/Est/Este:*
A Cafe, Douglas
14 North, Douglas
Alessandro's, Douglas
Bath & Bottle, Douglas
Costa, Douglas

Riley's, Douglas
Davison's Ice Cream Parlour, Douglas
The Ticket Hall, Douglas
Noble Hospital Hospital Cafe, Braddan
Fun Barn, Onchan
Inglewood Coffee & Cake, Douglas
Manx Telecon Shop, Douglas
Quids Inn, Douglas
Tower House, Douglas
Cafe Avanti, Douglas
Jaks Bar & Steak House, Douglas
77 Strand Street, Douglas
Creg ny Baa, TT Course
- *South/Süd/Sud/Sur:*
Cafe Delicious, Port Erin
Patchwork Cafe, Port St Mary
Silverdale Cafe, Ballasalla
Garrison, Castletown
The Sidings, Castletown
Whistle Stop Coffee Shop, Port Erin

🇬🇧 Healthcare

Make sure you're covered. All visitors to the Isle of Man need adequate insurance cover for any health care needs that may arise during their stay on the Island, including repatriation to their home country.

UK residents receive emergency-care free under a reciprocal agreement with the UK Government, but insurance to cover repatriation to the UK, if required, is still needed.

www.gov.im/health

▬ Gesundheitsschutz

Sorgen Sie für eine Krankenversicherung. Alle Besucher der Isle of Man müssen sicherstellen, dass sie über eine angemessene Krankenversicherung verfügen, die jegliche ggf. während des Aufenthalts auf der Insel nötige Krankenversorgung, einschließlich des Transports in das Heimatland, abdeckt.
Bürger des Vereinigten Königreichs erhalten eine kostenlose Notfallversorgung gemäß einem gegenseitigen Abkommen. Dennoch wird ggf. eine Versicherung benötigt, die den Rücktransport in das Vereinigte Königreich abdeckt.

■■ Santé

Assurez-vous d'être couverts. Tous les visiteurs de l'Île de Man ont besoin d'une couverture d'assurance suffisante pour prendre en charge les soins qui pourraient se produire lors de leur séjour sur l'île, rapatriement à leur pays d'origine inclus.
Les résidents du Royaume-Uni reçoivent des soins gratuits conformément à l'Accord réciproque sur la santé conclu avec le gouvernement du Royaume-Uni, mais une assurance couvrant le rapatriement au Royaume-Uni est encore nécessaire si requise.

■■ Asistencia Sanitaria

Compruebe si tiene cubierta la asistencia sanitaria. Todas las personas que visitan la Isla de Man requieren contar con un seguro que cubra las necesidades sanitarias que puedan surgir durante su estancia, incluyendo la repatriación a su país.
Los residentes en el Reino Unido reciben asistencia gratuita de urgencia en virtud del convenio recíproco suscrito con su gobierno; no obstante, deben disponer de un seguro que cubra la repatriación al Reino Unido en caso de necesidad.

DEU © 2016 Lily Publications Ltd. Jegliche Vervielfältigung ganz oder auszugsweise ist streng untersagt. Der vorliegende Inhalt basiert auf den zum Zeitpunkt der Nachforschung und Veröffentlichung verfügbaren Informationen. Die Herausgeber übernehmen keinerlei Haftung für die Veröffentlichung und die hierin enthaltenen Informationen. Verwender dieser Veröffentlichung, die die TT-Rennen, Southern 100 oder das Isle of Man Festival of Motorcycling (früher Manx Grand Prix) besuchen, tun dies auf eigene Gefahr. Weder Lily Publications noch andere an der Organisation der Rennen Beteiligte übernehmen dafür die Verantwortung oder Haftung. Die in dieser Veröffentlichung enthaltenen Karten wurden vom Herausgeber entworfen und gezeichnet und der Herausgeber gewährleistet deren Richtigkeit nicht. Wir empfehlen Lesern dringend, zusätzlich zu diesem Führer eine amtliche Karte zu verwenden.
Lily Publications haftet in keiner Weise für Schäden oder Verluste, die aus einem Besuch der in dieser Veröffentlichung beschriebenen oder aufgeführten Orte bzw. Attraktionen oder durch die Teilnahme an in diesem Führer beschriebenen oder aufgeführten Aktivitäten entstehen. Diese Bedingungen gelten nicht nur für die Isle of Man, sondern weltweit.

FR © 2016 Lily Publications Ltd. Toute reproduction partielle ou complète est strictement interdite. Le contenu du présent document repose sur les meilleurs renseignements disponibles au moment des recherches et de la publication. Les éditeurs déclinent toute responsabilité de quelque nature que ce soit suite à la publication et à l'égard des informations qui peuvent y figurer. Les personnes utilisant la présente publication qui viennent voir les courses TT, le Southern 100 ou le Festival de Moto de l'Île de Man (anciennement appelé le Manx Grand Prix) le font à leurs risques et périls, et ni Lily Productions, ni aucune autre partie associée à l'organisation des courses ne saurait être tenue responsable. Les cartes reproduites dans la présente publication ont été conçues et dessinées par l'éditeur et les éditeurs ne peuvent apporter aucune garantie quant à leur exactitude. Il est vivement conseillé aux lecteurs de se munir d'une carte du service cartographique de l'État parallèlement au présent guide pour de plus amples renseignements.
Lily Publications n'assume aucune responsabilité pour tous préjudices, dommages ou pertes consécutifs à la visite des lieux ou les attractions décrites ou listées dans la présente publication, ni pour tous préjudices, dommages ou pertes subis lors de la participation aux activités décrites ou listées dans le présent guide. Les présentes clauses ne s'appliquent pas uniquement à l'Île de Man mais à l'échelle mondiale.

ESP © 2016 Lily Publications Ltd. Queda rigurosamente prohibida la reproducción total o parcial de esta publicación. El contenido aquí presentado refleja la información más completa existente en el momento de su recopilación y publicación. La editorial no asume responsabilidad alguna en relación con la publicación o el material utilizado. Los asistentes al TT Races, a la Southern 100 o al Isle of Man Festival of Motorcycling (denominado anteriormente Manx Grand Prix) que utilicen esta publicación lo hacen bajo su propia responsabilidad, ni el virtud, Lily Publications y cualesquiera terceros relacionados con la organización de las carreras no asumen ningún tipo de responsabilidad. El diseño y la elaboración de los mapas incluidos en esta publicación corresponden a la editorial y esta no ofrece garantía de ningún tipo en cuanto a su exactitud. Se recomienda encarecidamente a los lectores que, conjuntamente con esta guía, utilicen un mapa de la agencia británica de cartografía Ordnance Survey con fines de consulta.
Lily Publications no se hace responsable de las pérdidas, lesiones o perjuicios que puedan producirse en relación con las visitas realizadas a los lugares o puntos de interés que se describen o citan en esta publicación o que se deriven de la participación en cualesquiera de las actividades igualmente descritas o citadas en la guía. Las presentes disposiciones son válidas tanto para la Isla de Man como para el resto del mundo.

Motorcycle mechanics...

Motorradwerkatätten
Mécaniciens Moto
Mecánicos de Motos

Moto Syko
Port Way LN5, Balthane Industrial Estate,
Ballasalla. IM9 2AJ
07624 459866
Servicing, repairs, tuning and accessories

LS Motorcycles
Mill Road, Peel.
07624 436429
Servicing, repairs and breakdown

tec
Andreas Airfield, Andreas. IM7 4JB
07624 414414
Repairs, bike brokers, spare parts, accessories
and breakdown

Road & Track Motor Cycles Ltd
Tynwald Street, Douglas. IM1 1BF
01624 623725
Servicing, repairs, accessories & new bikes

Paul Dedman Performance Ltd
The Showroom, North Shore Road, Ramsey.
01624 812390
Servicing, repairs, accessories, new bikes and
breakdown.

Isle of Man Honda
Highlander Garage, Kingswood Grove,
Douglas. IM1 3LY
01624 613000
Servicing, repairs, new bikes and accessories

Jason Griffiths Motorcycles Ltd
Optical House, Balthane Industrial Estate,
Ballasalla. IM9 2AH
01624 825940
Servicing, repairs, accessories and new bikes.

DSC Ltd T/A The Works
Shipyard Road, Ramsey. IM8 3DT
01624 845245
Repairs, spare parts and breakdown

Evomoto Ltd
Unit 1B, Gladstone Park Industrial Estate,
Ramsey. IM8 2LA
01624 819212
Repairs, servicing and accessories

Padgett's Motorcycles Sales
Victoria Garage, Victoria Road, Douglas, IM2
4HE
01624 673141
Repairs, new bikes and accessories

Campsites **and** Bunkhouses
Campingplätze **und** Schlafbaracken
Campings **et** Dortoirs
Campings **y** Albergues

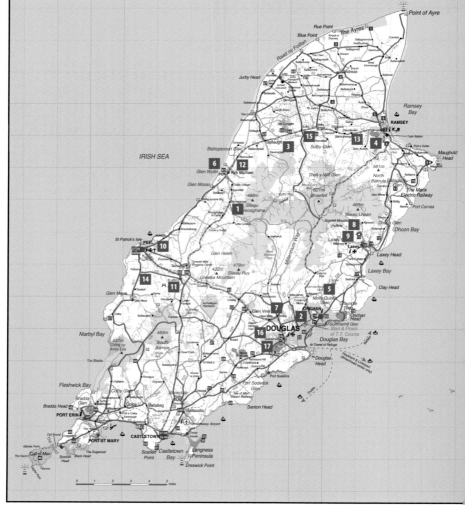

Campsites and Bunkhouses

Cronk Aashen Campsite – All Year
Barregaroo, Kirk Michael, Isle of Man IM6
?Q
www.cronkaashen.co.uk

Ballacottier Campsite – All Year
Ballacottier Road, Onchan, Isle of Man IM4
?Q
www.ukcampsite.co.uk

Ballamoar Campsite – TT and FOM only.
Ballamoar Farm, Ballaugh Glen, Ballaugh, Isle
? Man IM7 5EE
www.ukcampsite.co.uk

Crossags Campsite – April to September
Crossags Lane, Ramsey, Isle of Man IM8 2TB

Glen Dhoo Camping Site – TT and FOM
?ly
?ilberry, Onchan, near Douglas, Isle of Man
?M4 5BJ
www.ukcampsite.co.uk

Glen Wyllin Campsite – April to
?ptember
?len Wyllin, Kirk Michael, Isle of Man IM6
?AL

Glenlough Campsite – April – September
?allahutchin Hill, Union Mills, Isle of Man
?M4 4AT
www.glenloughcampsite.com

Laxey Campsite – Easter to September
?uarry Road, Laxey, Isle of Man IM4 7DU
www.laxey.org/camspite.html

9. **Laxey AFC Campsite – TT only**
Glen Road, Laxey, Isle of Man IM4 7AN
www.ukcampsite.co.uk

10. **Peel Camping Park – April to September**
Derby Road, Peel, Isle of Man IM5 1RG
www.peelonline.net

11. **St Johns Football Club Campsite – All Year**
Mullen E Cloie, Foxdale Road, St Johns, Isle of
Man IM4 3AR
www.ukcampsite.co.uk

12. **Michael United AFC – TT only**
Balleira Road, Kirk Michael, Isle of Man IM4
7AN
www.ukcampsite.co.uk

13. **Silly Moos Campsite – May to September**
Ballakillingan Farm, Churchtown, Isle of Man
IM8 2TB

14. **Upper Room Bunkhouse**
Knockaloe Beg Farm, Patrick, Isle of Man
IM5 3AQ
www.knockaloebegfarm.com

15. **Sulby Claddaghs Campsite – April September**
Sulby

16. **Douglas Rugby Club – TT only**
Quarter Bridge, Douglas, Isle of Man

17. **St. Georges Football Club Camp Site – TT Only**
Glencrutchery Road, Douglas, Isle of Man
IM2 6AN

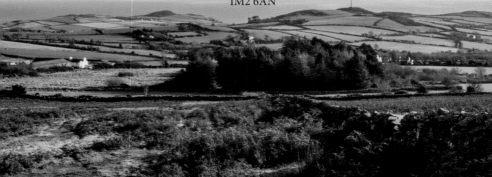

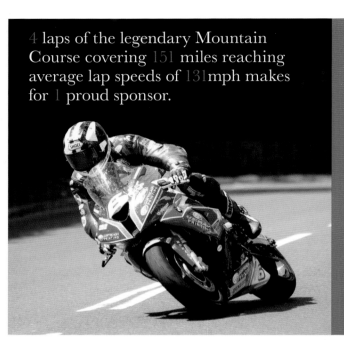
Deliciously Manx!

The Isle of Man has a rapidly growing international reputation for its outstanding food and drink. Traditionally known for its excellent kippers, the Island also boasts some of the finest seafood anywhere. With the Island being free from intensive farming methods, the quality of the produce is second to none – Loaghtan sheep provide lamb of the highest quality, while the distinctive taste of the Island's milk and cream is reflected in its award-winning dairy products.

The Island Kitchen illustrates the high standard of cuisine that can be found on the Isle of Man, showcasing signature dishes from the Island's finest chefs and restaurants using the abundant, high-quality produce that the Island is renowned for. From succulent starters to delicious desserts, you are sure to find a favourite and keep coming back for more.

RRP £19.95, 288 pages full colour.

Order securely online www.lilypublications.co.uk or telephone 01624 898446